Parenting Rewired

of related interest

Developing Differently
A Guide for Parents of Young Children with Autism, Intellectual
Disability, or Global Developmental Delay
Dr Joshua Muggleton
ISBN 978 1 78775 997 8
eISBN 978 1 78775 998 5

Spectrum Women—Autism and Parenting
Renata Jurkevythz, Maura Campbell and Lisa Morgan
ISBN 978 1 78775 294 8
eISBN 978 1 78775 295 5

Fifteen Things They Forgot to Tell You About Autism
The Stuff That Transformed My Life as an Autism Parent
Debby Elley
ISBN 978 1 78592 438 5
eISBN 978 1 78450 810 4

Coming Home to Autism
A Room-by-Room Approach to Supporting Your Child at Home after ASD Diagnosis
Tara Leniston and Rhian Grounds
ISBN 978 1 78592 436 1
eISBN 978 1 78450 808 1

Talking with Your Child about Their Autism Diagnosis
A Guide for Parents
Raelene Dundon
ISBN 978 1 78592 277 0
eISBN 978 1 78450 577 6

PARENTING REWIRED

How to Raise a Happy Autistic Child in a Very Neurotypical World

DANIELLE PUNTER
and
CHARLOTTE CHANEY

Jessica Kingsley Publishers
London and Philadelphia

First published in Great Britain in 2022 by Jessica Kingsley Publishers
An imprint of Hodder & Stoughton Ltd
An Hachette Company

3

A CIP catalogue record for this title is available from the
British Library and the Library of Congress

ISBN 978 1 83997 072 6
eISBN 978 1 83997 073 3

Printed and bound by CPI Group (UK) Ltd, Croydon, CR0 4YY

Jessica Kingsley Publishers' policy is to use papers that are natural,
renewable and recyclable products and made from wood grown in
sustainable forests. The logging and manufacturing processes are expected
to conform to the environmental regulations of the country of origin.

Jessica Kingsley Publishers
Carmelite House
50 Victoria Embankment
London EC4Y 0DZ

www.jkp.com

For Kiddo and Pie
who teach and inspire us daily.

Contents

INTRODUCTION

About three years ago when my son, whom we shall call "Kiddo" through-out this book, was finally settled in a school environment that was right for him, I had an urge to write a book. I had already been blogging for about a year and had found that by putting my own experiences into words I was able to help other people process their feelings and give some guidance for people on where to look for help. The same question came time and time again: "Have you got a book you can recommend for me?" People just starting out on their journey were desperate for clear, informative guidance as well as what I perceived to be a virtual hug from someone who had been through the transition from parenting in a neurotypical manner to an autistic one. If you're reading this now and this sounds like you, welcome. I know the saying "the grass isn't always greener on the other side" resonates with many, encouraging them to stay put. Well not in this case and not for you, because this time the grass really *is* greener on the other side and this book will show you how to start moving your way over from processing a child's behaviour and communication in a neurotypical manner to an autistic one. This book will teach you a new language, a different way to view the world that contains more richness than you could ever have imagined. Perhaps your child is already there and is diagnosed as autistic and you are desperately trying to find your way into their world. Don't worry because help is here in this book, together with a few drops of humour to help you along the way.

My name is Danielle, and as I write this I am 37 years old. It was only this year that I was finally diagnosed with attention deficit hyperactivity disorder (ADHD). I am on the never-ending waiting list for an autism assessment, but my ADHD assessment has shown that my ADHD affects my brain and processing in all but a very few areas of my life. My diagnosis was a lightbulb moment that shone across times in my life when I had significantly struggled. Like many autistic women and those with ADHD, I had been diagnosed with generalized anxiety disorder and depression in my teenage years. No consideration was given to what was really causing these issues and my struggles were put down to academic pressures. Throughout my life episodes of anxiety and depression have resurfaced and taken control. I was treated for those with medication and therapies, but something still felt wrong, like a part of me had been ignored. Nevertheless, I went to university and completed a psychology degree, which has helped me more in the last decade than I ever could have known.

When my son came along I began to realize how similar we were, as did my husband. Kiddo is now seven and currently thriving in life. It has taken a lot of fighting to get to this point. I've had times of exhaustion and desperation and learnt many things the hard way when perhaps I didn't need to, which is one of the reasons this book came about. Kiddo has several diagnoses, including autism, ADHD, sensory processing difficulties and a sleep disorder. He clearly suffers with anxiety like his mum, living in a neurotypical world that often does not cater for his needs. We live at home with Kiddo's dad and my husband, the only neurotypical in the house. Balancing everyone's needs is a challenging task we face daily.

When I first spoke with our editor about writing a book, I explained that the book I had always wanted was nowhere to be found when Kiddo was young. Instead of one book with an introduction to the changes we needed to make, the viewpoints on living with autism I craved and the practical things I could do to help my son were scattered across hundreds of books, each with its own pearl of wisdom. What's more, the majority were written by neurotypical people. So, the idea of this book was born: a book to help and give comfort to those neurotypical parents just starting their journey with an autistic child. We hope this book makes you feel safe and not alone. Be warned though – it will challenge you!

Knowing I was not neurotypical but not yet having a diagnosis, I knew I couldn't write this book alone. A book from only one viewpoint would also be hypocritical. There are so many different ways to view things as every autistic person is completely different. There needed to be a team of us, all of different ages, different autistic profiles and at different points on the parenting timeline. So, I approached two other people to help me.

I met Charlotte about three years ago whilst researching the possibility of getting an autism assistance dog. We were two people without any formal autism or ADHD diagnosis who just seemed to understand each other. As time went on and Charlotte met Kiddo, she told me about her son, whom we shall call Pie in this book. He was born at 23 weeks gestation with a range of challenges ahead of him. The staff took kindly to him and after a consultant called him "Pumpkin Pie" one day when he was wearing a baby grow with pumpkins on, Pie became a much-loved nickname for one of the fiercest children I have ever known.

Here she introduces herself and why she wanted to help write this book:

"I was diagnosed with dyslexia, dyspraxia and a speech and language disorder during my first year at school. The report stated that I would have been diagnosed with autism too, had I been a boy. I knew I didn't fit in to the world and was diagnosed with depression and anxiety as a teenager. I didn't get my diagnosis of autism and ADHD until adulthood. Music was where I saw my life but when my son (whom we shall call Pie) arrived at 23 weeks gestation, a career as a classical musician was not a possibility. Instead, I did a degree in religion and history when he was in hospital as an infant.

I taught part time for 12 years, but I still felt unfulfilled, and I knew that having a child with Pie's needs as well as my own diagnoses gave me a unique perspective on neurodiversity. In 2018 I became joint director of an assistance dog organization, and this was giving me a sense of fulfilment as I felt I was being able to use my experiences to help others. Since then I have also started a masters degree in autism as I felt I needed to have a more scientific understanding of autism to support my own personal experiences.

I know that all mothers say they are proud of their children, but Pie is quite literally my superhero. He is happy that his experiences are hopefully going to help other children. When he was born at 23 weeks gestation there was no talk of the future; we literally lived hour by hour. By defying the odds numerous times there have been occasions when he has appeared an enigma to those working with him. To me though he is Pie, not a list of diagnoses. However, to give an idea of where my advice is coming from it is good to give a little more background. Pie has too many diagnoses to list and explain but the ones that impact most of my parenting decisions are intellectual disability, acquired brain injury, multiple forms of epilepsy, Ehlers-Danlos syndrome, developmental coordination disorder, short gut syndrome which has left him doubly incontinent, hypothyroidism and of course autism and ADHD. He also has a complex mental health illness requiring treatment at a national centre. Despite all this Pie is a kind, loving, courageous, cheeky and determined 16-and-a-half-year-old. He is my very own Peter Pan and will happily play or watch programmes aimed at a much younger audience because the familiarity gives him so much joy. He adores animals and hopes to have a career working with animals.

When Danielle mentioned writing this book I was filled with dread as it would involve not only writing but also collaborative work, neither of which were a strong point for me. But it has been an exciting adventure and it turns out our autistic brains work quite well together!"

Looking back now I see how narrow my view of autism was; after all I only had my son's autism as an example. Charlotte opened my eyes as to how broad the spectrum is and how different people deal with different traits. Her insight, as you will read throughout this book, was absolutely mind-blowing and she helped me grow from someone with a limited view of what autism was to someone who realizes that I must always ask about an autistic child. How could I possibly know about their autism and how it affects them? Everyone is unique. It was this broadening of my knowledge that ultimately led me to pursue my own diagnosis.

Even with two of us now writing the book, I still didn't feel that was enough. We needed a different perspective.

Naomi is 12 and one of a set of twins, both autistic, both with incredibly different profiles. Her mother is a writer and blogger, and as Naomi has grown older she has been writing her own pieces on being autistic and growing up in a predominantly neurotypical world. She wrote this to introduce herself:

"My name is Naomi. I am 12 years old. I have a twin brother called Isaac and I live with my mum and dad in Scotland. Everyone in my family is autistic except my mum but we are all very different, because really everyone is different anyway. I help look after my brother because he has a lot of things that mean he needs a lot of care. I might be just 12 but I have done a lot of things. When I was younger, I wrote to get a suitable swing for my brother in the park as they didn't think about disabled children like him. I talk to my mum about lots of things and she writes it down so others know what life is like for me and I love making images to show people what autism is like for me and my brother and my dad. Having autism makes me a little different but it makes me awesome too."

The view of a young person should always be central when talking about how disability affects people, and Naomi has contributed some of her articles to show the world how we can help and also understand the struggles she faces.

So that's us and this is our book. We hope it comforts you but also challenges you. Challenges you to view the world through another person's eyes. Challenges you to reconsider habits, demands and principles that only suit a neurotypical world. If you open yourself up and humble yourself, your life will change beyond recognition. Happy reading.

CHAPTER 1

WHAT IS AUTISM?

To really understand what autism is, you need a little bit of background about how it was originally defined and how it has progressed up until this point in time. Part of the problem is that people learn about autism through the grapevine and don't always read the source themselves. This is how outdated definitions and versions of what autism is fly around social media in particular. So, let's start with what the actual word autism means.

Some background

The word autism has its roots in Ancient Greek from "autos" meaning "self". The term "autism" was first used by a Swiss psychiatrist, Eugen Bleuler, back in 1908 to describe a group of schizophrenic patients who were withdrawn and "self-absorbed". The term was then used in the 1940s by the eminent psychologists Leo Kanner and Hans Asperger. It was not until 1980 that the term autism was more widely used. Initially in 1980 it was described as "infantile autism", and then in 1987 the description was broadened to "autism disorder".

Nowadays clinicians use one of two books to assess individuals who may be autistic. In the UK the most commonly used manual is the *International Classification of Diseases* (ICD), whilst in the United States it is the *Diagnostic and Statistical Manual of Mental Disorders* (DSM). Both manuals tend to align closely in their definitions and diagnostic criteria, so throughout this book we will be referring to the DSM purely because their most up-to-date version (DSM-5) is available,[1] whereas the ICD won't be updated until 2022. The new ICD will very closely align with the current DSM.

According to the DSM-5, autism spectrum disorder is classified as a neurodevelopmental disorder. This is *not* the same as a mental health

---

1. APA, 2013

disorder, which is a very common myth that many people seem to believe. Before 2013, the autism diagnostic criteria were based on what was known as the "triad of impairment". This meant that in order to get a diagnosis the individual needed to demonstrate difficulties with social communication, difficulties with social interaction and inflexibility in activities and interests. In 2013 the triad became a dyad, combining social communication with impaired interaction.

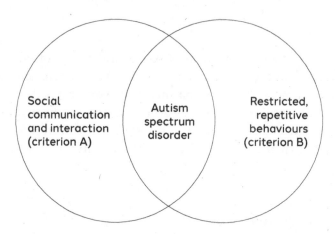

The required attributes of autism spectrum disorder are:

1. Persistent impairment in reciprocal social communication and social interaction (criterion A).
2. Restrictive, repetitive patterns of behaviour, interests or activities (criterion B).

These symptoms are present from early childhood and limit or impair everyday functioning. The Manual then continues to describe criteria C and D, which talk about how A and B impact that individual in daily life.

The DSM-5 also states that there should be either hypo or hyper sensitivity in sensory aspects of the environment. This may result in an individual being unable to tolerate (hypo) or craving (hyper) certain sounds, visual stimuli, smells or materials. These symptoms may be obvious from an early age or may be hidden until social demands overwhelm the person, for example, starting school or becoming a teenager where fashion, perfumes or concerts are more frequent experiences. Sensory challenges must cause clinically significant impairment in social or occupational areas of functioning. You can read more about this in Chapter 5 – "Sensory Processing".

The diagnosis should specify whether or not the individual's autism is accompanied by an intellectual impairment and/or a language disorder. This is a really important point because so many parents self-diagnose their child with autism when perhaps they only have a language impairment. The DSM-5 clearly states that both these things may accompany an autism diagnosis if present, but that both impaired social communication and interaction *and* restrictive, repetitive behaviours and interests *must* be present to be diagnosed as autistic. Language impairment alone is not enough and does not indicate autism.

What makes an autistic brain different from a neurotypical brain?

In short, they're just wired differently. The easiest way to show you this is with this illustration.

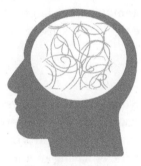 

Neurotypical brain   Autistic brain

Autistic brains are part of a group called neurodivergent brains. Autistic means you have a different brain structure to neurotypical people who make up the majority of the population (hence the word "typical"). Having an autistic brain leads to differences in social understanding, communication, sensory experiences and a whole lot more. In addition to autism there are a number of other neurodivergent conditions, including ADHD and dyslexia.

For years, being autistic has been viewed by many as an illness that requires a cure. What the illustration above shows is that it is not an illness or disease; rather it is simply a different way of thinking. Neurotypicals think in wavy lines; autistic people think in straight lines.

That's just an example of how the neural pathways in our brains can differ; what the actual brain structures look like is far more complex. It is important to understand that people are born autistic. They do not acquire a new brain structure over time that causes autism. It is part of our genetic makeup. Acquired brain injury may mean that individuals have huge sensory difficulties depending on which part of the brain was damaged, but this is not the same as autism, which you are born with. The main points to take away here are:

- You are born autistic. It is not due to "bad parenting", vaccines or other external factors.
- An autistic brain is simply wired differently to the majority of the population, changing how they experience the world around them.
- Autism is not a medical condition or illness. It can't and does not need to be cured.
- Every autistic individual is different. Their brains are not the same and so each person presents differently. Where one person may struggle hugely with verbal communication, another may not. However, that person may have significant sensory issues.

What autism is not

In order to understand what autism is, you also have to understand what it is not. So often different terms and diagnoses are used incorrectly and interchangeably with autism, which confuses which parts of a person's needs are actually caused by being autistic or having another diagnosis altogether. Autism is associated with mental health conditions, learning disabilities and learning difficulties, which often leads to misunderstandings of which symptoms relate to which diagnosis. So, before we continue any further, we are going to clearly define some of these co-morbid conditions so there is no confusion over what symptoms are autism and what symptoms are due to another condition entirely. We thought the easiest way to do this was in a table.

Condition or illness	Why it is different from autism	Symptoms that overlap with autism	Treatments
Depression	It is an illness, not a difference in brain structure	Repetitive behaviour Social withdrawal Rumination Difficulty eating Difficulty sleeping	Medication Therapies such as cognitive behavioural therapy (CBT) (this must be adapted to the individual and their usual baseline of behaviour taken into account)
Anxiety disorder	It is a psychiatric disorder that involves extreme fear or worry	Social anxiety Panic attacks Fear or worry	Medication Therapies such as CBT (this must be adapted to the individual and their usual baseline of behaviour taken into account)
Intellectual disability	This is diagnosed when a person has a low IQ (less than 70). Autism alone does not impact upon a person's IQ	Difficulty with everyday tasks Taking longer to process, learn and develop new skills	No treatment is required, just extra support
Learning difficulties (also known as learning disabilities in the USA)	These do not affect general intellect.[2] They are conditions that affect the rate and ease for someone to gain and understand knowledge as quickly as their peers. They include dyslexia, dyspraxia, dyscalculia and ADHD	Difficulty with everyday tasks Taking longer to process, learn and develop new skills	Many require additional support in a classroom or learning environment or, in the case of ADHD, possible medication

cont.

---

2   Mencap, n.d.

Condition or illness	Why it is different from autism	Symptoms that overlap with autism	Treatments
ADHD	An impairment of the brain's executive functions. Includes inattention, weak impulse control, hyperactivity and problems with organizing tasks	Difficulty with social interactions, sensory difficulties, can struggle with eye contact	ADHD can be treated with medication and specific therapies that help with organization, planning and executing tasks
Eating disorders	A mental health condition where one uses "the control of food to cope with feelings and situations"[3]	Rigidity in routines Desire for social acceptance Focus on small details Struggles with food textures	Specialist therapy

This is by no means an exhaustive list. What it illustrates is how common it is for an autistic person to suffer from a number of illnesses and conditions at the same time as being autistic. What we must not do is use autism as an umbrella diagnosis for all these conditions because then people miss out on the appropriate treatment and are left to suffer under the premise that their symptoms are due to their autism.

What is essential when treating or supporting autistic people for any of the conditions above, or any others for that matter, is modifying therapies and taking into account the individual's autism to make sure that particular therapy is appropriate. All people respond differently to therapies. I had two years of psychotherapy and made zero progress. I had one session of hypnotherapy and it changed my entire life.

When a very well-meaning professional become aware of Pie's anxiety, she eagerly embarked on a mindfulness session. The previous week she had been on a course as the local authority special education needs (SEN) team were eager to put mindfulness into the children's curriculum. The session began with Pie being handed a chocolate button and being told to suck and savour the taste. Within a matter of seconds Pie was choking and gagging as he didn't have the motor control to do this and quickly his chocolate heaven became a total disaster. Undeterred by this, the professional quickly moved on and told Pie to imagine relaxing on a beach. Like many individuals on the spectrum, Pie has limited imagination skills

---

3   NHS, 2021

and could not grasp the concept at all. This quickly developed into an anxious meltdown. When he had calmed down he was asked to evaluate the session, to which he promptly responded, "a waste of time".

Mindfulness was a totally inappropriate therapy for Pie. It was not risk assessed and his autism was not considered. That's not to say that mindfulness is not for any autistic person, but the individual's needs must be taken into account when any kind of therapy for an additional condition is suggested.

What should have happened is that Pie should have been considered as an individual. No two autistic people are exactly the same. There is a well-known saying: "If you've met one person with autism, you've met one person with autism." Each autistic person is unique. With this in mind, it is important to appreciate that not all the same support mechanisms or techniques will help all autistic people. Not only are no two people the same, but also all autistic people lie at different points on the autism spectrum.

When you mention the word spectrum, most people will think of a straight line:

"mild autism" ←——————————→ "severe autism"

The assumption is that individuals lie somewhere along this line/spectrum according to their abilities. In short, it is total and utter nonsense. You may have heard people say, "Well we are all a little bit on the spectrum." No. No we are not. You are either diagnosed autistic or you are not. It's a common misconception that ADHD lies on the autism spectrum. This is not true. In the same way, you either have ADHD or you don't. What is true is that autism and ADHD share a lot of the same symptoms and having one of these diagnoses increases the chance of also having the other.

The areas of the autism spectrum

So, if the straight-line illustration above does not correctly represent the autism spectrum, what does the spectrum look like? Autism has many contributing factors. There are numerous areas of characteristics that give a person their individual autistic profile. The chart below demonstrates some of these characteristics. If you search the web you will find many different interpretations of the spectrum in this style. This is our version for the purposes of illustrating how each person is different only; it should not be used as a conclusive assessment of any kind.

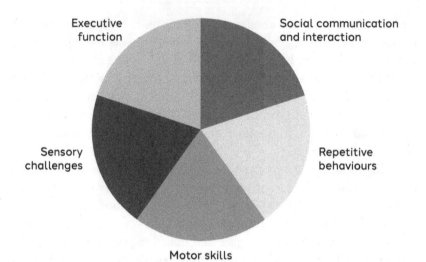

The autism spectrum is made up of several areas such as those listed in the chart above. Each individual is scored on how much that particular area affects them in their daily life and their scores are charted to produce a visual representation of their autistic profile. For example, the diagrams that follow show Kiddo's profile (first) versus Pie's profile (second). They both have an autism diagnosis, but the way their autism affects them could not be more different in all areas except for repetitive behaviour. A score near the centre of the graph would mean relatively little difficulty. A score towards the outside means significant difficulties in everyday life.

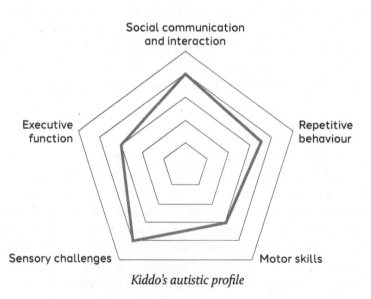

Kiddo's autistic profile

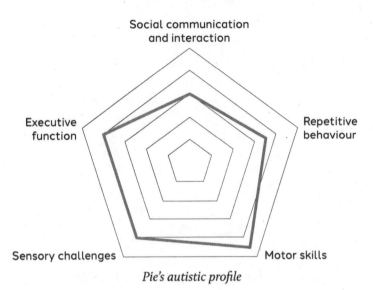

Pie's autistic profile

The two profiles look very different yet both Kiddo and Pie have a diagnosis of autism.

Many people believe that once these scores are given, a person's profile stays static for life. This couldn't be further from the truth. Autistic profiles can actually change on a daily basis depending on the environment that the person finds themselves in. For example, school days present a whole host of different challenges to non-school days. On a school day there may be far more sensory challenges, motor skills challenges and need for executive function (planning and organizing). A non-school day may not have these pressures, but the lack of structure may make it much harder to socially interact when you can spend the whole day relaxing in your bedroom. Most people usually need this time to recuperate and whilst appearing a lot more antisocial and as though they are not making an effort, they are actually recharging their batteries in their safe environment. Without this down time they cannot function at school or work throughout the week. If we compare Kiddo's profiles on a school day and non-school day, you can clearly see the difference in the profile he presents to the outside world:

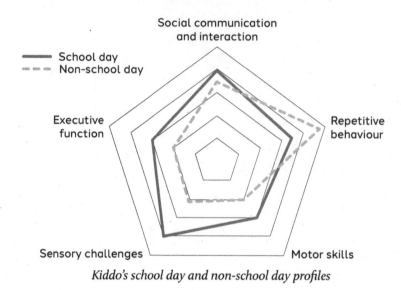

Kiddo's school day and non-school day profiles

On a school day Kiddo has considerably more sensory challenges and finds using his executive function a little harder. This isn't surprising given the number of people he is around and how much extra pressure is placed on his sensory receptors. When he is at home and not with large numbers of people, Kiddo finds it easier to communicate verbally and has far fewer sensory challenges because we have engineered our house that way. He does, however, engage in far more repetitive behaviours because he can, and this is essential for him to recuperate from the week at school.

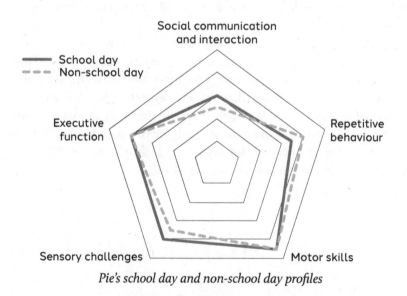

Pie's school day and non-school day profiles

Pie's profile doesn't actually change that much, and this is because he is home tutored. His environment does not change except for the presence of his tutor. In comparison to Kiddo, who attends a special school, we can see how Pie is able to maintain a more consistent profile. School days exhaust his social communication and interaction more due to interacting with his teacher, but what we see here is just how big a factor environment is in how an autistic person may feel.

Pie wasn't always home tutored; he attended a school environment for many years. Charlotte also scored Pie on days when he had attended a school environment, and in the chart below we see how much Pie struggled with studying in a busy environment compared to when he was at home with his tutor.

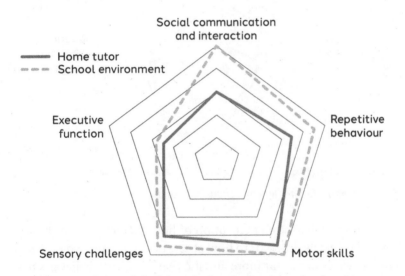

Pie's presentation of challenges he faced when in a school environment

This shows how Pie's symptoms were hugely exacerbated in the school environment. Whilst attending a special needs school, his motor skills became so impaired that he sat inside a cupboard all day unable to walk, and he did not want to leave it. He could not communicate verbally, and his sensory challenges, repetitive behaviour and executive function were all more severe. The school environment was not one that Pie could tolerate or flourish in. Whilst Kiddo shows a change in profile, this is not because he struggles to the same extent that Pie did. Kiddo has challenges that his staff are aware of and together we support him to find ways he can cope with, and most of all enjoy, his school life. He skips in every morning, usually dragging his staff member behind him as he is so keen to get on. As long as he gets his recovery time at home then he loves it.

Another interesting point to cover is how an autistic person views the effects of their autism profile versus how a neurotypical person views it. As an experiment we asked Charlotte to assess herself and a close family friend of hers to assess her using our spectrum categories. The chart below shows how Charlotte thinks she presents to the outside world compared to the experience of her close friend.

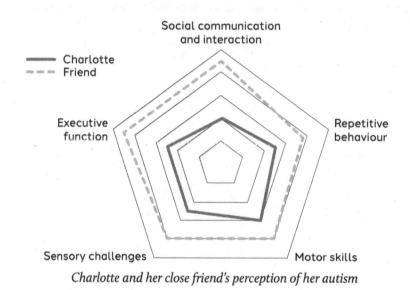

Charlotte and her close friend's perception of her autism

As you can see, Charlotte's perception of how she presents to the outside world is hugely different to how others do. Her neurotypical friend essentially views her as far more autistic than Charlotte believes she is. When speaking to them both it became apparent that Charlotte does not value the same types of social interactions that neurotypical people do. Her friend marked her as presenting as struggling with social communication, whereas Charlotte didn't feel she had a problem with that at all. Upon questioning this further it was discovered that this is because her neurotypical friend places far more value on facial expressions and body language to communicate, whereas Charlotte prioritizes words. Charlotte has excellent verbal language skills so marked herself as not having much difficulty. Her friend felt Charlotte was really struggling in this area. What it all comes down to is how much we value certain things and how these values differ between neurotypicals and autistics. There is no right or wrong, just differences.

Masking

This can also be the other way round though. Masking is when a child or adult who is autistic hides their symptoms, characteristics, stims and tics etc. from the outside world in order to fit in and not be noticed. In Charlotte's case, she feels completely at ease with her close friend and so presents very naturally as herself. But what happens when she or someone masks?

Although I am not yet diagnosed autistic, I am diagnosed ADHD and in the same way as those with autism, those diagnosed with ADHD mask their true feelings and struggles so they fit in with the outside world. So here is my ADHD profile as a teenager that I presented to the outside world versus how I felt inside. I have changed the characteristics slightly for ADHD, but the principles remain the same.

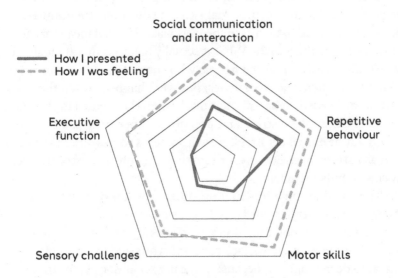

How I presented vs how I was feeling

The difference in how I presented myself in school and how I was feeling is stark. I didn't cause any problems in school. When I came home though I was short tempered, just wanted to watch TV to relax and would be in bed early to recover from the day. When I reached 17, the effect of keeping up the persona in the chart caught up with me and became too much, and I had breakdown. I was unable to leave the house and I barely left my room. I couldn't tolerate having any lights on and only lit candles. I didn't want to socialize, I refused school and the idea of stepping outside our front door gave me such serious anxiety attacks that I would have to be medicated so I fell asleep in order to calm and recover from them. And this is why the use of functioning labels is such a problem.

Charlotte is also a master masker. We have both used it as a survival technique over the years to get through periods of life where we didn't want to be seen as different, and this is where functioning labels play a very dangerous part in underestimating the effects that keeping up appearances can cause.

High functioning and low functioning autism

The term "high functioning" is often used to describe an autistic person who is able to function independently in a mainstream society without a problem, as their autism doesn't affect their day-to-day life that much. This is a very dangerous misunderstanding. Just because an autistic person seems able to cope in a mainstream education environment or not require many adjustments in the workplace does not mean that their autism does not affect them. What it actually means is that their autism doesn't affect *you* and all the people who spend time with them such as friends, teachers and workmates. But what happens when the "high functioning" autistic takes off their mask when they return to their safe space? All the anxiety, stress and pressure of appearing calm in what can actually be extremely stressful environments comes out. Meltdowns occur as a stress release and very often they are only witnessed by a very few close family members.

The belief that "high functioning" autistic people don't need help in school, work or everyday life is completely false. Teachers will often say, "They're fine in school, they don't need sensory breaks etc." Actually, they do. Underneath the surface constant stress and anxiety chip away at an autistic person. Just because you can't see it doesn't mean it isn't there. Adjustments, sensory breaks and structure should all be put in place if asked for. Without these, the build-up of constant pressure and anxiety of holding in how they really feel can lead to serious mental health problems in the future. Support must be put in place from very early on in any environment where the person says they need it. "High functioning" does not mean a person is okay. It simply means that other people aren't affected by their autism and support for this person should not be dismissed because they appear not to need it.

There is also a term used to describe autistic people who are less able to communicate and have poor motor skills and severe sensory challenges. "Low functioning" is used to describe autistic people who show obvious signs on a daily basis of being autistic. They need constant support and may attend special schools or be unable to work. With this label we have the opposite problem. "Low functioning" is often associated with a low IQ or learning disability. So often we see children who are given this label written off at a very young age. Phrases like, "they will never talk" or "they will never use the toilet" or "they will never work" are thrown around in the early years and quite frankly it is often complete rubbish. Autistic children develop at their own pace. By giving them a label such as "low functioning", you run the risk that people will never consider them for any potential. This is false. Kiddo has been described as both high and low functioning and do you know what? He is neither. At age seven his verbal communication is still very limited and he does not speak in full sentences, but wow what a brain this child has! He taught himself to read by age four, taught himself to write and taught himself all his times tables up to 12 by age seven. We were told so many things in the early years, but we just encourage him to be whoever he is meant to be.

The functioning labels are inaccurate: they generalize and they focus only on how other people are affected by that person's autism, not how that person's autism affects them.

Are you autistic or do you have autism?

Terminology is constantly debated for autism and that is simply because each person has a right to determine for themselves how they would like to be referred to. There is however a good analogy as to why people prefer to be called autistic.

Autism describes a neurological difference. It is how a person's brain is wired. For many people they feel that this means that their autism is so innate and such a part of who they are that they don't want autism to be referred to as something additional that they carry around with them. This image illustrates how many autistic people feel when someone refers to them as "having autism". It is as though they are carrying around a bag full of autism as an accessory, and they find this offensive as autism is a part of who they are. After all, you wouldn't say "someone with  homosexuality" would you? No, because it is a part of who they are.

On the flip side there are many people who actually prefer the term "has autism". This is because they don't want to be defined by their autism. They feel it is only a small part of who they are and that many more parts of their personality contribute to their overall person. People who have multiple diagnoses may not want to be defined by one of their diagnoses. They are not ashamed of their autism; some simply prefer to be recognized as having other characteristics as well. So, Julie may be good at sport, an excellent artist, enjoy reading and have autism. John is autistic, enjoys music, plays the guitar really well and loves his writing.

The most important thing is that you ask the person how they would like to be referred to, as it is their decision. There are large groups and online movements of people who request that they are called "autistic". This should be respected when referring to them. We so often hear of people attending courses or training where they are told how to refer to autistic people. You can't learn these things from training; people should be allowed to choose for themselves.

There is a lot of debate about how to refer to your child, either as being autistic or having autism. If your child is able to discuss this, explain the two terms and let them decide. Perhaps they will change their mind at some point and that's okay. It's about empowering our children with both sides of the debate and allowing them to choose for themselves whilst not having a term forced upon them.

If your child is unable to have this discussion then obviously it becomes a little trickier. Kiddo isn't able to have this debate; Charlotte is. Charlotte has several diagnoses, as you will have seen from her introduction. She doesn't believe any one of them defines her more than the others. It's important that Charlotte is allowed to identify herself as she would like to. That is her right. For Kiddo, I tend to refer to him according to whichever diagnosis is more prevalent at the time, but I naturally say, "He is autistic." For me it's because having read the reasoning that we explained above elsewhere, it just sits more comfortably with me. If he is ever able to decide for himself with all the information, I shall follow his lead.

Obviously, we can't ask everyone who reads this book, so we will be using both terms throughout and say to our readers that we respect however you would like to be referred to.

Is autism a disability?

The final thing we would like to cover in this chapter is whether or not autism should be referred to as a disability. This is constantly debated and again this is because it is completely individual to each person and also each individual day.

Some people are diagnosed as autistic, but their traits do not stop them interacting with the wider world. They are aware they see things differently and are happy to be who they are living in a majority-led neurotypical world.

Some people can find their traits a challenge. Perhaps they struggle to verbalize language or have poor motor skills, making simple tasks much harder.

Some autistic people have much more pronounced traits and find everyday life and tasks extremely hard. Communication means they struggle to buy the correct items they need, sensory sensitivities are so acute that a trip on public transport just isn't possible and poor executive function may mean they cannot plan tasks to such an extent that they need help with personal care 24 hours a day.

The spectrum truly varies from person to person, making it so different for each of us. Just because seven-year-old Fred down the road can cope in mainstream education with just a few adjustments doesn't mean that seven-year-old Alice from up the road can cope in school at all.

On top of each person's autistic profile, you then have to consider how they're feeling that day. For example, Charlotte is fully verbal and can do everything from ordering a coffee to completing her masters degree. However, Charlotte has days where due to sensory overload and executive function problems she is nonverbal. On those days her autism would definitely be considered a disability. It is the same with ADHD. Some days you wouldn't know I have ADHD at all. On other days I am paralysed to the spot, unable to move or initiate any task whatsoever due to being so understimulated and my executive function being frozen. I wouldn't be able to go to work, complete any household tasks or even make a meal to eat. On those days my ADHD would be considered a disability.

So when people argue over whether autism is a disability or not, it is simply because their experiences of being autistic or having children on the spectrum vary so greatly. So, is autism a disability? The answer is, it can be...

CHAPTER RECAP

- Autism is a lifelong condition and there is no cure.
- Autism on its own is *not* a learning or intellectual disability.
- Autism is diagnosed according to strict criteria.
- Autistic people are not all geniuses.
- Autism is *not* caused by bad parenting.

CHAPTER 2

STARTING FROM SCRATCH

The question we get asked the most by parents who are new to autism is, "What do I do first?" Our answer is always the same and is possibly the most important thing you will ever do as a parent of an autistic child.

Humble yourself. Forget every practical thing you thought you knew about parenting, because whilst it works for neurotypical children, it won't necessarily work for an autistic child. Every single autistic person is different. Many families with more than one child on the spectrum will often talk of how different each of their children's needs are or how their sensory profiles clash. This book cannot tell you exactly what *your* child needs but it can give you the tools to work that out whilst covering the most encountered challenges of raising an autistic child in a very neurotypical world.

To be suddenly told your child will follow a different developmental path in life can be really overwhelming, especially if you have little or no experience of neurodiversity. The aim of this book is to help you understand the differences between autistic and neurotypical brains and how your parenting may need to change to meet the needs of your child(ren).

Learn to understand your child

So if you are to humble yourself and be prepared to learn new parenting techniques, who should you listen to? There is a plethora of professionals, parents, autistic adults and experts on autism in this world. However, there is one person who you must listen to above everyone else. Your child.

So often we see parents complaining that they don't know what their child wants or how they feel. If their child isn't talking yet then how can the parent possibly know what they need? To truly understand your child you will need to learn a whole new language. Their language. They may not be using words, but they are showing you what they like and dislike every day. When Kiddo was two years old he was nonverbal. He absolutely hated it when people sang along to songs or music on the TV. He couldn't politely say, "Excuse me, Mum, but I find it awfully troublesome when you sing along with *Thomas the Tank Engine*." He couldn't even say, "No!" So instead he routinely punched me in the face. Every time I sang he would hit me. It didn't take us long to realize that the act of hitting was his nonverbal way of saying, "Please stop! Your singing is too much input for my brain whilst the TV is on too!" I'm pretty sure he just hated my singing too to be honest, and still does to this day. So we stopped singing along to TV theme tunes and the violence subsided. It seems like such a simple thing when you read about it, but frequently what we see is the child being disciplined for hitting and no attempt to work out the reason why. Yes, hitting needs to stop and it is an important lesson to be learnt. But when your child is unable to communicate, or struggling at that time, and hitting you because they are in anguish, you must consider whether full-blown punishment is necessary when really all they are desperately trying to do is communicate with you. Learning what your child's actions mean will take time. Seven years in and I am still learning every day. Over the years though I have started to read Kiddo's body language, see the warning signs of when he is struggling and even work out which behaviour relates to a specific problem. For example, if Kiddo begins to destroy furniture or property at home, he is in physical pain. From keeping a very simple diary we saw that painkillers were what eventually calmed him down after destructive behaviour in that particular way. Painkillers didn't work for other types of destruction such as self-harm. He was communicating with us and showing us what he needed. Nowadays he has associated the giving of painkillers with the pain easing and will say "medicine" some of the time. Learn to read your child.

Another thing we hear oh so frequently is, "But all children love this. I know I did when I was a child!" But does your child have the same brain structure as you? Do they experience senses the same way you do? Are noises painfully loud? Are smells hugely overwhelming? Is listening to multiple conversations too chaotic for their brain to handle? Previously we talked about what having a different brain structure means when out and about in the real world. Just because most children enjoy something doesn't mean your child will. Just because you enjoyed something as a child doesn't mean your child will. So often we see parents taking their children to soft play and their child is screaming. "I just don't understand, all children love soft play!" the parent or carer will say. No, they don't. There are a whole range of reasons why your child may be distressed, and we will cover those in later chapters. What you must get rid of though is the assumption that because other children are enjoying something, or you enjoyed something as a child, your child will enjoy it too. An autistic brain will experience a situation or environment in a completely different way to a neurotypical one.

The disappointment a parent feels when their expectation of enjoyment isn't met because a child doesn't adore a particular experience can be devastating. I know; I feel it sometimes and that is okay. But (and this is a big "but"), you must remember that these expectations you have for parenthood and life experiences are not the fault of your child. Children don't read a manual whilst in the womb or on the adoption register that tells them exactly what their future parents would like them to be or do in order to make them happy. Children are born into this world as individuals, as who they are supposed to be. Our job as parents or carers is not to change them but to nurture who they really are. To guide them through the world, whether it is set up for them to succeed easily or not. To see where they may need more support, or perhaps where their talents are so incredible and encourage them to pursue them, however unconventional they may be. To fight against those who feel that they need curing and that the only way to be in this world is to be just like everybody else. All the resistance we see that parents show in truly accepting an autistic child comes from pre-set expectations. So where do we get these from?

From the day you even start to consider that you might want to be a parent, you suddenly become bombarded by media messages on having children. Of course, they have been there all along but it's only when you start to contemplate such a massive life change that you start taking more notice. Magazines, TV adverts, antenatal classes: they all talk you through a variety of topics. The most common are nappies, clothes, furniture, birthing plans and pain relief during labour. Glossy photos of families at Disneyland, the huge Christmas dinner set up, your child's first day at school. It's all there laid out in front of us. This is how your family will be. Our expectations are hugely moulded by the mainstream media because they want us to spend money. Then there are our own childhood experiences. Whether we had a fabulous childhood or not, most of us have an opinion on whether we want the same for our children or the very opposite. More expectation becomes engrained within us. This is a lot for your little bundle of joy to live up to. It is a huge weight that any child of any age will hold on their shoulders. So, if before you started reading this book you felt you didn't have any expectations for your child in life, we urge you to think again and consider what assumptions (however subconscious) you've held about the life your child is going to lead. It is here that we must start from scratch.

The only way to help your child fulfil their incredible potential is to understand their needs and ignore what everyone else thinks they need. Autistic children are among the most intelligent in the world. They are hugely creative and extremely talented and provide a view on life that neurotypical people could never imagine. Yet many assume they have little potential, that they will not excel academically and that they won't achieve the same goals as their peers. Why? Because we expect them to follow the same developmental and academic paths as everyone else. We tell them they must fit into a system that is not designed for them. We believe our autistic children are not academically capable because they are placed in schools where the environment prevents them from learning. Einstein said, "Everybody is a genius, but if you judge a fish by its ability to climb a tree it will spend its whole life believing that it is stupid." Autistic children require different environments to learn in than neurotypical children do; they need different methods of teaching and communication. Kiddo couldn't function in a mainstream school environment at all, yet he taught himself to read by age four all on his own. Why do we force our children to fit into these systems? Because it is our expectation. We don't realize that choosing a different option to the masses is not a bad thing. So, having discussed our subconscious expectations for our children, when do we consciously start comparing our children to "the norm"? The answer is as soon as they are born.

The problem with neurotypical developmental milestones

Up until the point you give birth, it is likely you haven't considered that your child may be autistic. Perhaps if you have adopted an autistic child you have been given some information at this point. So along comes your child and you assume they will follow a detailed developmental progression, so much so that in the UK you're given a book on it. The red book. Now in some cases, such a premature babies, you may be spoken to about autism and other neuro disabilities very early on. Charlotte was given a lot of information about ADHD, autism and other disabilities when

Pie was born because he was so premature. Whereas whilst Kiddo was a week premature, he was considered healthy, so I was given absolutely no information at all. Yet we were both given the same red book.

For those who are unfamiliar with it, the red book details growth charts, developmental checklists, trends, behaviours we should be seeing, the lot. The idea is to use it as a tool to identify any delays, deficits or problems that may arise. It is used as the absolute be-all and end-all when it comes to your child developing "correctly", and whilst we do need some kind of comparison so we can spot whether our children are autistic or not, this book instead simply tells us that if our child doesn't tick every box, they are not normal.

When Pie had his six-week check, Charlotte was so proud that he had survived from such a premature birth. It was an unbelievable achievement and one that Charlotte was immensely proud of. Along came the professional to conduct the check, who opened the red book and said, "He has failed every single one of these milestones." In Charlotte's eyes though, he hadn't. He had achieved more than was ever originally thought. More than any doctor or nurse could have predicted. He is 16 and a half as I write this and a happy young man who enjoys horse riding, trains and working with animals. Yet the red book marked him as a failure.

When I took Kiddo for his two-year check, I already knew he was supposedly functioning at a six-month-old's level in most areas. He was indeed referred for further assessment and it was that day I took the red book and shoved it in a drawer. I never opened it again. I wasn't interested in what my child could or couldn't do in comparison to his peers because they were no longer his peers. He was clearly not neurotypical and all I was being asked constantly was what he could and couldn't do. The comparison to other children, the expectations from the book, the expectations from the media: it all brought me tumbling down. Until I realized that Kiddo was like a fish being compared to a monkey. He wasn't born to travel the same path as neurotypicals. He wasn't born to achieve the same things either. He was born to do so much more, and that was the point where typical milestones were thrown out of the window for me.

Developmental milestones are written for neurotypically developing children: for children who all develop in the same way, at the same pace and in a straight, linear fashion. Our advice to you is to forget these milestones and the timeline when they supposedly occur. They are not written for your child. You will spend every waking minute trying to make them do things that they will find utterly pointless and most likely make them not want to interact with you. Instead, focus on what your child is interested in. If you don't know how to do this yet, then start by playing with the same objects as them at the same time. Copy their playing and movements. Don't interfere with what they are doing; just quietly play alongside them, copying what they do. If you're playing with spoons, quietly hand them a spoon and see if they take it. See if they hand it back. Playtime may look very different, and we will discuss this later on in the book, but remember this key message. It is not your child's duty to learn how to engage in your world. It's your duty to learn how to engage in theirs.

Autistic children meet milestones all the time, but they are completely individual to that child. They won't match more typical milestones; they won't match other autistic children's ones either. They will be beautifully personal to your child and your child alone. What's more, you get to decide what milestones you want to remember too.

I can remember the first time Kiddo walked at 16 months; I can remember the first time he crawled at almost 10 months. But do you know which milestone I remember above them all? The first time I said, "Find your shoes please Kiddo", and he went and actually found them. I didn't expect him to react to my request at all, he never did. I kept going every day and one day, when he was over three years old, I walked round the corner to see him standing by the coat rack holding his shoes. I made such a fuss of him, and his smile could have stretched to the end of the road and back. I dropped him at preschool and when I came home, I cried. The joy of him completing such a simple task was more important to me than any milestone written in the red book. More important than anything he was "supposed" to do according to professionals. As he grew up, some milestones stayed hugely simple such as the ability to tolerate wearing a T-shirt to school. Some milestones were way above his age range, such as learning all his times tables to 12 by the time he was seven. In some respects he is now so far ahead of the game. In others he is much further behind. It doesn't matter; we just celebrate everything he does because he works so hard at it. Only if he wants to, of course. He is still my son after all. If there is no motivation, you won't see huge amounts of progress in Kiddo because he has decided it is not worth the effort.

Many parents though still complain of the upset caused by their child not following the typical developmental curve brings. Why? Because of well-meaning, concerned fellow parents who are worried something is wrong with your child. Or interfering, misinformed, ignorant people, whichever you prefer to call them. When you have an autistic child, comparison is your biggest enemy. Remember what we said right at the beginning of this chapter: no two autistic people are the same. None. Even if they have the exact same sensory profile, there will still be differences. So, if your child is a unique, one-off autistic, how can you possibly compare them to anyone? You can't. The comparison doesn't exist. It would be like comparing the way a dog and a fish swims, or how an elephant or a cheetah runs. There is no comparison; it's not possible. Other parents however may not understand this, and that is where the problem lies. In well-meaning advice.

Over the years of having to listen to this well-meaning advice, we understand how it can really drag you down: lots of suggestions of things to try or ways to manage behaviour that you either know won't work, or you give it a go and it is a complete disaster. Somehow you need to be able to let this advice wash over you and remain confident in your ability as a parent. That's no easy task and we often have parents or carers asking us how we actually do this when it comes to our own children. So, here is some practical advice for dealing with (hopefully) well-meaning people who wish to offer their words of wisdom to you about their own neurotypical child.

1. Prepare a verbal script that you can use as a response every time someone tells you how to parent your child. Now the reason for having a fixed response is because it is more successful in preventing a full-blown debate opening up. Nowadays I'm up for the debate because I know I will win it; however when Kiddo was two years old I was confused and my confidence in my parenting skills was at an all-time low. I just couldn't handle quotes from Gina Ford's parenting books so I developed a comeback phrase. It varied from day to day, but usually it was something along the lines of, "Thanks, but things are a little different for us. I'll look it up later." Then I changed the subject.

2. Tell them that if they're interested in how autistic children develop, you would be happy to send them some articles. Or recommend a book (ahem). This is a good one for family members and close friends as they usually have a genuine interest in helping the child develop healthy relationships and want to understand why you as the main caregiver are parenting a little differently. If they tell you not to worry about it, then that's usually a sign that point number 3 might need to be considered.

3. Ask yourself if you are in the right social circle for you and your child. Are you being supported? Are you being believed? Do you

want to attend these meet-ups or do they make you feel anxious? This can be a really hard step to take as many people have been friends with their parent circle for a long time. These groups are adored by parents as they bring common ground to laugh over, cry over and support each other over. If this isn't happening, you may need to find a new crowd. We aren't saying that you need to immediately cut out all your friends and start again only with families who have autistic children. What we are saying is that you need to make sure you are surrounded by families who make you feel good about yourself, understand your challenges and can offer advice that may actually work. Be vigilant of those groups who are trying to change their child into a neurotypical one with therapies such as ABA (applied behaviour analysis); that's not what we are suggesting. Find people who celebrate their child for who they really are. Search for blogs by autistic adults and join their support groups. Attend local meet-ups and judge for yourself whether people are celebrating their children for who they really are. It might be work to start with, but when you find them your whole world will change. Find your tribe.

As well as ignoring others' opinions on your parenting, there is one other thing we recommend you build a thick skin for. The Stare. We've all seen the struggling parent dealing with their toddler having a tantrum in the middle of a crowded public place. We have all been that person too, I have no doubt. When our children are young, tantrums are accepted by society. You get supportive looks from other parents and probably the odd tut from someone who thinks they can parent their toddler better than you in that very second. You shrug it off. As your children get older though, it becomes a different story.

Your child is bigger, older and according to society should know better. The wider public are also lacking one other key piece of information: the difference between a tantrum and an autistic meltdown. We will discuss this later in the book, but the point is that when your child is suffering from sensory overload, society just sees a child at the age that should know better having a tantrum. Cue The Stare. My God, it can shoot through you like a dagger, cold as ice, ripping every piece of self-confidence you have to shreds along the way. The Stare has sent me running to my car with Kiddo, caused me tears that people don't understand my son and I'm pretty sure was responsible for a fair amount of weight gain through comfort eating. But that's not the way to go people, not at all.

The reality is that we live in a society that doesn't widely understand autism. It also has no desire to learn about it unless that person is personally affected by it in some way. When you realize that the people who are judging you often know very little about autism, it becomes easier to discount their opinions of your parenting methods.

This is where we recommend that you start to build that thick skin. Over the years Charlotte and I have forgotten those "Stares". In time I started answering back to people when they made comments or gave disapproving looks. It takes inner strength to continually take your child out into a world that is designed to cause them stress. You make as many changes as you can for them to help them build positive experiences and yet still you are met by resistance from the wider world. There is only one thing that will help you build that thick skin: confidence that you are doing the right thing for your child. We hope that by the end of this book your skin will be a lot thicker than it was when you started reading. Find that confidence inside yourself; let the rest of the world make judgements on situations they don't understand. It's only you and your child that truly matter.

"Giving in" to autism

The last thing we wanted to mention in this chapter is a notion that hopefully we have already covered somewhat. It's the idea that by changing the way you play, socialize and educate your child you are "giving in" to autism. We hear it in many situations, including, "I'm not sending them to a special needs school, I'm not giving in" or "I'm not going to stop taking them to restaurants on a Saturday night, that's just giving in." What exactly are you giving in to? We see parents who are so determined not to make any adjustments to the way they live their life. They will continue as they always have; after all their child will adjust eventuality. It's really important though to try to remember that autistic people may need and want a very different life to neurotypical people, and that's okay. Here are a few questions you can ask yourself that might help you work out how you're feeling.

1. Are you refusing to make changes in your life because you feel it is best for your child, or best for you? The fear of change does crazy things to people; it makes us blind to what is happening right in

front of us. You may be worried about losing friends, changing the way you socialize or embracing a new education system, but have you considered the needs of your child? Have you thought about the emotional scars you are causing them each time you take them somewhere the sound is too loud or the lights are too bright? Of course, there will be times where you want to try new things or go places. Keeping the new challenge at a pace your child can cope with, and with plenty of support in place, will help them grow and become confident they can trust you to help them.

2. Is your child in the right environment for them to learn? Some will prefer a mainstream school, some will need a special school and others may not flourish in a school environment at all. It's a myth that sending your child to a special school means you are giving up on them. It could be the best decision you ever make. Look at what's working for your child in school and what is not. This will help you look objectively at whether they are in the right learning environment for them.

3. Are you worried about losing your social circle because your child finds meeting up with them very distressing? This is normal. Of course you don't want to lose friends. Perhaps your child will adjust if you keep going? It's important to be aware that your child may be learning to mask their behaviours and fit in. They will still feel the anxiety they did when you continue to meet up ten years down the line. Perhaps your child will develop coping mechanisms from negative experiences. We all want our children to flourish but having to learn to cope in a situation is very different from enjoying a situation and learning positively from it. What is essential is that you choose a group of people, a place and a time that can accommodate your child's needs. If your friends don't want to meet in such a place, perhaps it's time to search for friends with children with similar needs. You don't have to cut anyone out of your life; just make sure that socializing is a positive experience for your child should you choose to do it.

A so called "normal" life and a neurotypical life are two very different things. The only reason people call it normal is down to the fact that it's the life the majority of people lead. Nothing more. By attaching the word "normal" to "neurotypical" you immediately suggest to yourself and everyone else around you that anyone who is not neurotypical is in fact abnormal. This isn't true and it is not a healthy perspective to have. Just because something is different to a majority doesn't make it abnormal; it just makes it different to the majority. Those words mean exactly what they say. Your child isn't abnormal, but they do need things done in a different way. Removing the word "normal" from your daily life is hard to do, so we suggest you define your own "normal" and commit to it. It's the only way you will find true happiness.

CHAPTER RECAP

- Understanding your child will unlock their full potential.
- Autistic brains process the world around them very differently to neurotypical brains.
- Be proud of your child and take time to explain their need to others.
- Be flexible; often small adaptations can make the most difference.
- Define your own "normal".

CHAPTER 3

PARENTING PRINCIPLES

Since every autistic person is completely individual, this book can't give you exact answers on how to parent your child. There are areas and topics in which many parents frequently experience challenges, and we have dedicated specific chapters to those in this book. For the rest of your parenting though, you will need to judge the needs of your child. In order to help you do this, we have come up with some key guiding principles that will help you consider any action you need to take. They are in no particular order of importance. We hope you find them helpful.

Follow your child's lead

We have already talked about learning to read your child and noticing subtle (or not so subtle) signals that may mean they are in distress, in pain, hungry or enjoying themselves! The next thing to do is go with it. Now obviously there are times when it is not possible or appropriate to give yourself to their wants, because we must go to work and school etc. This principle is of particular importance in social situations such as days out, trips to attractions and visits to see family and friends. If you start to notice signs that your child may be starting to become overwhelmed, stressed or upset, that is the time to act. Do not leave it until they are in full-blown meltdown. This doesn't mean you need to leave someone's house straight away; it may just mean that they need a quiet space so they don't become dysregulated. Remember, neurotypical children struggle to communicate emotions, let alone a child who may not even have verbal communication yet. It is our responsibility to interpret those signs and act accordingly, not for the child to work out what they need and do it. As your child grows older you will notice they may be able to self-regulate more and tell you what they need. You still need to be committed to following their lead though, otherwise why would they bother telling you? Waiting to the point where your child reaches meltdown is too late. Yes, sometimes meltdowns come on extremely quickly and without warning; you won't always get it right. By following their lead you will prevent negative experiences in environments they find challenging and they will be more encouraged to try again in the future, which brings us nicely on to the next principle.

Earn their trust

All children learn about the world by having a point of safety, venturing out away from it and knowing that when it all gets too much they can come back to that safety at any point. This helps them gauge what is safe in the world and what is not. It gives them the opportunity to try to experience new things. For autistic children the world is an even scarier place. Senses are heightened and experiences are more vivid and intense. This means that there is far more opportunity for an autistic child to become overwhelmed and to need to search for that place of safety. When they are very young, their parents or carers are their place of safety. Perhaps as they grow older it will be a tent or a room that is their safe space where they can fully relax from perceived threats. What happens though when they don't have an adult who they can trust to help them and support them in difficult environments? They either refuse to explore and become attached to that person (or refuse to leave their safe space), or they experience a huge number of meltdowns because they know this is a guaranteed way to get you to remove them from a painful environment. Building that relationship of trust is key to accessing the outside world. Show your child that you understand experiences must be introduced slowly. Show them, perhaps on a day where their senses are particularly hyped, that you understand how painful it is for them. Show them that you will follow their lead and end activities or outings early and that it is okay. This foundation of trust will open up so many doors for you in the future.

Learn the difference between a tantrum and a meltdown

The word meltdown is hugely overused in parenting. Quite often parents and the media use it to describe very loud or active tantrums, but in reality a meltdown and a tantrum couldn't be more different. The way the two words are used interchangeably can be extremely confusing, especially for parents who are just starting to learn about autism. The way you parent a tantrum or a meltdown also could not be more different, so it is important to learn the differences so you can apply the right parenting technique.

The main difference between a tantrum and a meltdown is that tantrums have a purpose. The child is in control of their actions and has an end goal they want to achieve with their behaviour. Whether they are determined that it isn't time for bed yet or whether they are trying to embarrass you in a shop until you give in and buy that toy they want, a tantrum is a behavioural act with a purpose in mind. A meltdown may incorrectly be perceived as a behaviour where the child is attempting to get their own way; however it is actually the result of overload in the brain. This could include too much input from physical senses such as light, sound or touch but also can include situations where the brain is having to work too hard to keep up with processing verbal information that is trying to get in. The term "information overload" means exactly what it says, only for autistic people it can tip them into a meltdown as the brain simply has to work too hard to comprehend all the information trying to get in.

But how do you spot the difference? As well as understanding why tantrums and meltdowns are different there are also some physical and behavioural signs to look for that will help you decipher which is happening. The following behaviours can be seen in each one.

Tantrum	Meltdown
Has a purpose or target that the behaviour is trying to achieve	The child is not trying to achieve any purpose or outcome with their behaviour
Makes sure the adult is watching and paying attention	They are not concerned by whether or not an adult is paying attention
Can engage in conversation or nonverbal reasoning (such as bribes etc.)	They cannot engage in any kind of communication, verbal or otherwise
Can be distracted by a new activity	No amount of distraction or bribery can calm them
Does not self-harm or inflict pain on themselves	Owing to a lack of awareness of their environment, they may sustain an unintentional injury
Calms after a reasonable amount of time	A meltdown can last any amount of time but can often occur for 30 minutes or more

Something else to consider is the possibility of a tantrum triggering a meltdown. There is no doubt that a child with a very definite objective in mind can become extremely angry if they are denied it. The more tenacious and stubborn they are, the more likely they are to put a considerable amount of effort into a tantrum. What happens though when the energy, passion and effort put into a tantrum actually causes a meltdown? It can be really difficult to identify when what was originally a tantrum becomes a meltdown. All the emotion of a tantrum is a lot for a little (or big) autistic brain to process, and in a lot of cases it tips the brain from a controlled tantrum to an unavoidable and uncontrolled meltdown. The more you learn to read your child the more you will begin to spot warning signs that the tantrum is changing. This is effectively your last chance to use distraction in order to avoid a full-blown meltdown. Once the meltdown has started you will no longer be able to distract, and your priority will be to keep your child safe from harm. This is even more difficult when it happens in public.

I know this from personal experience, and it was always my worst nightmare. Picture this. You're sitting in a lovely play cafe drinking coffee and chatting with other parents. From the corner of your eye you see that another child is playing with a toy your child wants. You go over and explain they must wait their turn. (Ha! Ever had to try to make an autistic child wait?) Obviously they're not impressed and start having a tantrum. You take the right approach and tell them they can't have the toy yet, but the tantrum gets louder and more animated and you start noticing familiar signs. A meltdown is on the horizon. In just a few moments your child will be attempting self-harm and you will have lost the opportunity to communicate with them. Not wanting to draw attention to yourself and to prevent harm to your child, you take your last chance for distraction and offer to buy them an ice cream. It works and your child dutifully follows you to the counter. You did it! It's then you notice The Stare. It's coming at you from every angle as you walk to the counter. You doubt your parenting ability and whether you called this correctly. You question whether your child is simply spoiled by you and the damage you might be doing if you have got this wrong. We have one thing to say to every parent in this situation:

Everyone else can sod off.

You know your child, you know what you have prevented and you know that now you can communicate with your child at a reasonable level. Be confident in the decisions you make and keep working on that thick skin we have already talked about.

Make changes slowly

Autistic people find any kind of change, no matter how small, challenging and need time to adjust. Often what we see is people saying they have only made a small change to a routine and their child has really struggled to process it. There are two really common problems we come across when parents or carers make changes to routines, environments or pre-made plans. The first is that more than one thing has changed. For example, say you had planned to go to the beach. Your child has pictured the beach, knows what type of clothes they need to wear and what sights, sounds, textures and smells to expect. On the morning you had planned to go the beach it rains, and you decide that you will go to a really nice restaurant for lunch instead. Thinking this is a lovely treat for your children, you tell them the location has changed and you're leaving in ten minutes. Cue meltdown. In the neurotypical person's head only one thing has changed: the location. Here is what has changed in the autistic person's head:

- the place
- the clothing
- the journey
- the sights
- the sounds
- the smells
- the textures
- the activities.

They have only ten minutes to process this, and their brain can't handle all the new information that this change in plans brings with it. They need time to adjust calmly. There are occasions where last-minute plans can be changed positively, and let's face it, everyday plans change all the time. The trick is to replace the activity that you had originally planned with one that your child simply adores, has done many times before and knows exactly what to expect. Hello McDonald's! A trip somewhere familiar is safe and with no surprises so the child doesn't need time to adjust. If you still wish to go out and do something a little different then try to choose an activity that is related to what would have happened at the beach. At the beach there would have been swimming and ice cream so perhaps go to a local pool and get ice cream on the way home. Give your child time to prepare for this though as it is still a change. Bear in mind how many factors your child is planning for because it will never simply be "the beach".

Planning for eventualities is a real challenge for families with autistic children. No matter how much you plan, there will always be times when you need to go places or do things that you can't plan for. This is a part of life. That doesn't mean that there is nothing you can do to support your child when things don't go to plan. Here's Charlotte on how she has approached this with Pie:

"Pie would have long periods of being quite poorly and sometimes immunity issues meant that he would not be able to go out for weeks at a time with no warning. This meant that there were lots of changes to plans and his routine. When it became clear that this would be a reoccurring pattern, I added a question mark symbol to his schedule so that there would be a planned but unknown part to his day. Sometimes we would swap things around as a gentle way to help him learn to adjust. This was not easy for Pie, but it was a skill he needed to learn so we stuck at it and gave him lots of support. It was easier to support him in accepting changes when it was not essential, and this then meant that he learnt to adapt to the unexpected. That isn't to say that it doesn't bother him; he still finds it hard to adjust, but he has a strategy and we can work through it."

Charlotte prefers to think of a routine like a flexible bandage rather than a rigid plaster cast. The plaster cast has no room for the limb to move, as this is what is needed initially to begin the healing process. As the person recovers, they still need to have support but one that offers some room to move. It can seem scary for caregivers and autistic children alike to move from the protection of a plaster cast, but in the long term it is best to do this in a gradual and controlled way with the knowledge that you can return to more rigid options at a later time.

The second problem we encounter is that children (or adults) are not given enough time to contemplate these changes. How much processing time is needed will depend on the child and how much change is intended in the routine or outing. The more changes there are happening, the more time a child needs to process them. If you're in a situation where a child needs an immediate change to prevent an accident, then first make the physical changes to the environment to keep them safe before beginning to change the actual routine. Never underestimate how much time a small change will take to become embedded in a routine. If the change is accepted quickly, then great. So many things can affect how quickly a change becomes comfortable practice: how tired the child is, how calm they have felt during the day previously or how important the routine stage you're changing is to them. However long it takes, be calm and be patient. These changes are hard work. The brain fires up and produces a lot of adrenaline over such things and can send a person into fight or flight. Help them feel safe and supported in a calm environment and you will notice that they accept changes far more quickly.

Allow them to progress when the time is right for them

We have previously mentioned the red book and how it outlines a typical developmental plan for neurotypical children. Now you know not to panic about supposed missed milestones; you have to learn to notice when your child may be ready for their own progression. This can be a hard step to accept, especially when many parents and carers around you are progressing at things all at the same pace. But here's the thing: forcing your child to progress in areas when they're not ready will get you absolutely nowhere and will be a complete waste of your time and effort. So, what should you be on the lookout for that shows your child is ready to progress in a certain skill or area? Let's take using cutlery as an example.

Kiddo and Pie both refused to use cutlery for a very long time. Why would they want to? It's just extra equipment and extra manoeuvres in order to get food from your plate into your mouth. Total waste of energy. At a time when neurotypical children their age were using them without a problem, neither of our children were interested in the slightest. So, here's what we did. When we laid the table we would only put the pieces of cutlery that were needed (we still cut their food up for them so no need for a knife, and quite frankly either of our children with a knife is an utterly terrifying thought). We carried on using our own cutlery and didn't make a fuss. As time went on they watched how we ate our food and whilst they were watching we would hold up the various pieces of cutlery and say "fork" or "spoon". One day Kiddo started to pick his fork up. He would try to use it but couldn't manage the coordination and gave up really easily. We praised him for trying but didn't force him to use it. As time went on it became less and less of an effort for him to use his fork. One day I forgot to put one out and he said, "Fork!" and wouldn't eat until he had it. He was five when he routinely used a fork and used it for his own meals. Many children are doing that by age three. It didn't matter though; he was eating and he progressed when the time was right for him. Pie was 15 when he started using cutlery routinely. For him to be able to control the movements and not be in pain, he needed a different style. When he requested cutlery, Charlotte tried many different types and they eventually found one that was suitable. She didn't push him; she allowed him to progress at his own pace.

The key is to look for signs of interest and offer opportunities rather than force them. If your child shows an immediate interest in something then perhaps they are ready to take the next step. If you offer them an opportunity to use a fork or use the toilet and they show zero interest then now isn't the right time. Going at your child's pace will prevent countless meltdowns and negative experiences, which will only push progress further and further away. We will talk about how this relates to toilet training in a later chapter.

Embrace their interests

When you want to form a relationship with someone, be it friendship, romance, business and so on, you usually have something in common that draws you together. Sometimes people will spark a new interest in you, and you will look into it more, maybe research it a bit and then you can engage in chatting socially or formally about the subject. The more you do it, the more the relationship grows and develops. It really isn't any different with autistic children. They have interests that you can learn about and become involved in just as much as the next person; it's just that maybe they're not the interests you would expect a child of that age to have. We've seen people try to draw a child's attention to toys and activities that they enjoyed as a child or that are advertised on TV. Maybe their friend's children absolutely love that toy, so why wouldn't their own? They make the huge mistake of trying to get the child to engage in toys and games that neurotypical children and neurotypical adults enjoy, and it doesn't work.

Back when Kiddo was 12 months old, I was childminding. I had all these fantastic activities lined up, including arts and crafts and games. The other children always engaged so well, but Kiddo was not interested at all. I remember one specific morning where I had laid out a sensory farm using different cereals for textures. The other children happily role played for over an hour. Not Kiddo. He saw the big silver spoon I had used to place the cereals on the farm and was absolutely captivated by it. He took the spoon and settled in another room by himself whilst he ran his fingers along the smooth edges, watched the shine change as he moved it around and banged it on different surfaces to see what noise it would make. Later that afternoon, after the other children had gone home, I got out a second big silver spoon and we sat together admiring them. He showed me so much detail I had never noticed before. We pointed them towards the sunlight to create reflections and banged them together to make a new sound. All children learn through play, but there is no set way in which that play has to happen. We only think that there is due to the mainstream media and the majority of the world being neurotypical. Six years on and Kiddo now brings me his iPad to show me what he has been building on his games because he knows I will take an interest in what he is doing. It transformed our relationship.

The same principle applies as our children grow older. Pie at the age of 16 is still hugely interested in *Thomas the Tank Engine*. Charlotte will often sit and watch episodes with him and talk about the characters. It doesn't matter what other children his age might be interested in; this is what Pie is interested in. Charlotte has always endured any interest Pie may have and it is one of the reasons their relationship is so strong.

At times it may seem like you have watched the same episode or played with the same spoon a million times. There is no doubt repetitive play can be dull if your brain isn't wired that way. Even if your brain is wired that way it can still be exceptionally hard to tolerate if it is not one of your own interests, but none of that really matters. Remind yourself why you do this and what your aim is. This is the building block for developing that meaningful relationship with your child. It's likely you're only used to developing relationships with people you have shared interests with; in the case of your child it doesn't matter. Stop trying to force them to be interested in what you *think* they should be and take a look at what they are actually showing an interest in.

Learn the difference between what they can't do and what they won't do

So often we see autistic children being penalized for not doing something they have been told to do. It can be something so simple that very often it is not considered whether the child can actually tolerate the task or whether they even know how to do it. Let's take a simple example of putting on your shoes to leave the house.

You ask your child to put their shoes on. Simple enough, yes? Ten minutes later they still haven't done it so you remind them, and this continues until half an hour after you first asked and they still aren't wearing their shoes. By this point your patience has faded and you most likely give the child a consequence: if they don't put their shoes on right now they don't get to go to wherever you were planning on going (which you know your child was really looking forward to). Your child still doesn't put their shoes on. The consequence is given, and the child is disappointed whilst you feel exasperated by them not completing such a simple task. Your immediate thought is, "Why won't they just put their shoes on?!"

What is rarely considered is whether they actually *can* put their shoes on that day. There are a number of reasons why they *can't* put their shoes on that could include any of the following:

1. They don't physically know how to carry out the task. Just because an autistic child has the executive function to know how to put their shoes on one day doesn't mean they will have it the next. Are they tired? Overwhelmed by the environment? Do they need a prompt on how to get started? Check whether they need support if they haven't popped their shoes on like they usually would.

2. Are they currently involved in another task? Autistic people find it very hard to transfer between tasks. Often the previous task has to be finished or has to be completed to a comfortable point (e.g. reading to the end of the current chapter in their book) before they can process the next task. Sudden changes or requests without warning make it more likely that the child hasn't finished the task they're engaged in – they might be racing to finish that section of their book so they can move on to the task of putting on their shoes. Did you give them enough warning and enough time to finish what they were doing?

3. Does your child find the particular shoes you have asked them to put on painful to wear? Sensory issues are a huge factor in whether or not an autistic person is able to carry out a task. Big changes can also mean they need time to adjust to the new feel of something. So, is it the first time they have worn wellies in months? Are their shoes too small now and need changing? Are they just having a day where all their senses are really sensitive, and that particular footwear isn't something they can tolerate? Maybe if footwear isn't a priority (if you're only going to another house or not leaving the car) they can choose some thick socks or their own choice of shoes? Does it really matter what they wear on their feet? Kiddo won't wear wellies very often at all so many a time I have taken spare trainers and socks with me, and when

he has finished jumping in puddles I dry him off and pop warm, dry shoes on. Is it really that big a deal?

When you are disciplined as a child for not doing something that you actually need support with it can be devastating. On the outside you may seem like a competent child who is just being resistant; on the inside you are screaming for help because you don't know why you can't do these things. Even now at age 37, there are evenings where it is my turn to make the evening meal and my husband will find me standing still in the middle of the kitchen because I quite literally don't know where to start. He doesn't shout at me; he helps me. Maybe we order takeaway. Learn the difference between when your child won't do something and when they simply can't. Obviously you won't get it right every time, but it is important that you consider this carefully to minimize any effect on your child.

Don't be held back by a diagnosis

A diagnosis of autism is not a reason to be held back or a reason to stop trying. It's there to help make you and other people aware that in order to help your child succeed they may need adjustments to be made for them. In some cases these adjustments will level the playing field with everyone else. In some cases it will improve their chances of achieving what they strive for. What is certain though is that if you or your child spend their lifetime living in their comfort zone, they will miss out on so much! We aren't saying you should force your child to try things they are clearly terrified of. What we are saying is as their parent or carer it is your job to support them into trying new things. Don't just drive them to the door of an extra-curricular club, dump them and leg it. That's not going to help anyone or build up your child's confidence. What you could do is arrange to meet the club staff outside of club hours first. Go and see the venue with no one else there. If there is music, ask them to play it so your child knows how loud it will be. Familiarize them with as much as possible first so that when their peers are there that's the only thing your child has to process and concentrate on. The social interaction. I remember joining a swimming club when I was 11 because my best friend wanted me to. We just went for a session one evening and it was utter hell on earth for me. I had so much to process. The smells, the sounds, the routine, the staff and the swimmers. It was completely overwhelming and after a few weeks I just couldn't handle it. If I had been to watch a session from afar, walked around the changing rooms, asked for some adjustments to be made and so on, I'm almost sure I would have stayed and really enjoyed it because I love swimming. Instead, no one knew why I stopped going.

If we had known at the time that I would self-diagnose as autistic later in life I have no doubt that someone outside our family would have said, "Oh, she couldn't cope because she was autistic." No, I couldn't cope because my anxiety got the better of me and the appropriate adjustments were never made. They couldn't have been as we didn't know about my self-diagnosed autism at the time. Having an early diagnosis is a gift, but only if you use it to help your child access the world, not avoid it.

CHAPTER RECAP

- Build up trust with your child.
- Learn to recognize the difference between a meltdown and a tantrum.
- Encourage your child to have interests and hobbies.
- Understand the difference between what your child can't do and what they won't do.
- Ensure you develop clear boundaries and that these are consistent between all the child's parents and caregivers.

CHAPTER 4

ASSESSMENT AND DIAGNOSIS

Before we begin the journey through the world of assessment, it is important to remember that it is an assessment to assess your child's development. It does not mean that the right outcome is an autism diagnosis. The assessment process is designed not only to look to see if the person reaches the threshold for a diagnosis but also to look at their development, and in some cases to rule out or confirm other diagnoses. Whatever the outcome of your child's assessment, the process can be very useful as it will flag up areas where support is needed and give suggestions of ways your child can be helped to overcome some of their challenges.

For many families there will have been a long journey prior to the start of the assessment process and for some there will have been many ups and downs to get their child's needs acknowledged. Sometimes when a child has previous medical and/or developmental difficulties, it may have been a professional who will have suggested that your child is assessed for autism. For some parents it may be a decision based upon personal feelings that your child needs an assessment; for others it may be a process that you are not yet ready to undertake or one that you feel is not necessary. Whatever your situation, don't panic as there is no right or wrong way to feel about this journey. What is certain though is that this decision will be based on several factors, and each will be unique to your situation. It is important that you never feel pushed into or away from having your child assessed for autism. You know your child better than anyone else.

As parents, we have both had completely different experiences of our sons being assessed and getting a diagnosis. When Kiddo was two I was asked why I wanted to label him as autistic. Despite not having anywhere near the knowledge I have now, I was knowledgeable enough to realize the importance of a diagnosis for a child who may encounter difficulties at school and in life in general. Unfortunately for the person who asked me this, my impulsivity got the better of me and I answered in the following way:

"Are you seriously asking me why my two-year-old who gets distressed on a daily basis, self-harms and is unable to communicate verbally needs support? Do you really think this boy will be able to get through school on his own? Or do you think I am making this up? And I'm not labelling him, thank you; I'm asking for a diagnosis so he can get the help and support he needs."

She looked a tad shocked. Looking backing on this many years later, I now see exactly what she meant. It is a really valid question and one we should all ask ourselves. The problem in this scenario was how she asked me. She wasn't looking at me, her body language looked completely disinterested and her tone of voice bordered on sarcastic. Had the question been phrased differently, I would have happily answered, "Because a diagnosis for this child is a doorway to the support he needs."

For Pie, autism was first mentioned when he was two. He was still in hospital and developmentally was severely delayed. His autism assessment happened in a somewhat organic way as doctors tried to explain his unconventional developmental profile. The outcome of these assessments was that he was autistic; however his lead paediatrician was concerned that having a confirmed diagnosis of autism may mean that it would hide other conditions. Shortly before his fifth birthday Pie received his diagnosis of autism because it was felt that it was the right time. If you had asked Charlotte up until a few years ago, she would have said that being diagnosed at that stage was the right thing to do. However, over the past few years it has become clear that his paediatrician who had her concerns was correct. He ended up with delayed diagnoses of his epileptic seizures, intellectual disability and acquired brain injury. Nobody is disputing Pie is autistic, but his diagnosis at the age of five did cover up some of the other challenges and delayed him receiving the help and treatment that he so desperately needed. Whilst we are talking about a child with an incredibly complex profile it is always worth evaluating a diagnosis's value even when it is being offered to you on a plate. Although it absolutely shouldn't, a formal diagnosis can overshadow other medical conditions and prevent necessary treatment from taking place.

I can remember being asked why I as an adult would like to be assessed for autism. I was told I was coping just fine, and it wouldn't make any difference to my daily life. When we asked for Kiddo to be assessed though, no one questioned it because they could see he wasn't coping in daily life. Statements like, "You've made it this far without a diagnosis" or "A diagnosis won't make any difference to the support you receive in school" are not helpful and are also irrelevant. Until a full written assessment has been conducted by the relevant professional, nobody can possibly comment on whether a diagnosis will be of any practical help. Absolutely no one but the person being assessed and/or their close family can comment on whether a diagnosis will be of any emotional help as well. So, before you begin the full assessment process, do a small self-assessment and ask yourself the following questions. Then you will be prepared to answer why you are pursuing a diagnosis and feel confident it is the right way forward for you and your family.

- Would a diagnosis provide evidence for more help in school/education?
- Would a diagnosis help you with your parenting and understanding how to meet your child's needs?
- Would a diagnosis help your child understand themselves more and possibly help with self-esteem and self-confidence?
- Would a diagnosis help you understand what adjustments need to be made at home so your child is happy and supported?
- Would a diagnosis help with lifelong support required in further education or the workplace?
- If your child has the appropriate level of understanding, is it something they want to do?

Obviously this isn't an exhaustive list, but it is a good way to check in with yourself and make sure you are clear on why you are pursuing this diagnosis. Write down your answers and keep them for when you are asked why you are wanting to join the waiting list.

It is important to remember that whilst an assessment and potential diagnosis can be an important resource in your tool kit, it isn't a solution. However, a diagnosis can give your child a feeling of self-worth and enable them to have an understanding of themselves, which will allow them to advocate better for themselves as they get older.

As the wider world becomes more aware of autism and more understanding, there is a wider knowledge of what to look out for. The internet is full of checklists and quizzes on whether you are autistic or not. This can be very helpful, but it can also be dangerous. People panic that seeing a couple of traits of autism means that their child is autistic.

Some autistic traits are also a part of normal development. For example, a toddler lining up their toys can be quite common. However, when this is done excessively, and at an older age, it then becomes atypical. Having so much information available at your fingertips can mean you begin looking for signs and symptoms. Try not to take these symptoms out of context too much. For a diagnosis to be given, certain symptoms must be constantly present and co-exist with other symptoms. It may be that your child has another condition or perhaps doesn't have a formal condition at all. The point is that no one should declare their child autistic based on one or two traits. Seek medical advice and assessment. We appreciate that some children, especially girls, may mask behaviours or may not display symptoms in an obvious way. This can make it much harder to obtain a diagnosis. There are professionals who specialize in this area that may be worth pursuing.

How to get an autism assessment

So, you have decided that you would like your child to undergo an assessment for autism. How do you go about this? The pathway of an autism assessment can differ between countries, states, counties and even organizations. The first thing we recommend is looking online to see if your local healthcare provider has placed any information on their website about how to go about this. For countries that use private health-care, companies should have clear procedure and costs. If you are in the UK and have chosen to go private to avoid waiting lists, it is essential that you check you are going through an assessment provider that is approved by your local authority. If you don't, the authority may refuse your private diagnosis and prevent you from using it to gain support in your child's education setting. You can challenge this legally, but it is much easier to use an approved service. Unfortunately, there are private practitioners out there who will assess without using a multi-agency approach. This means they diagnose based on one meeting with your child and do not collect observations or reports from other professionals who can provide valuable and essential insight. Whilst we appreciate many of you are searching for a diagnosis, the most important thing is that your assessment is done by a reputable healthcare provider who has excellent assessment methods and appreciates the need for a wide range of opinions in different environments. An incorrect diagnosis will cause your child huge difficulties and could actually limit their future possibilities. Sadly there are conditions placed on procedures, such as gaining permanent residency in Australia as an example,[1] where having an autism diagnosis can prevent you from doing this.

In the UK, many local authorities will have a list of private providers they will accept a diagnosis from for this very reason. A local authority has to have a good reason for not accepting a diagnosis, but you don't want this to be another battle, so we recommend checking with them about approved private providers or get it notified in writing that they will accept your diagnosis from the provider you have chosen.

If you're in the UK and using the NHS, your diagnosis pathway will depend on where you live and your child's age. If your child is not under a paediatrician, the first port of call for most people is their health visitor (for under fives) or your general practitioner (GP).

The first time you talk to a professional about your concerns it can be scary and overwhelming, so make sure you prepare in advance what you are going to say. Both Charlotte and I will always take along written notes. This is partly owing to Charlotte's own autism but also because she then knows it is presented in a format that is clear and factual. My ADHD can mean that I forget points and need to refer to a list to make sure I have covered all the ground I want to.

We would suggest separating out facts, figures and observations from emotion at this point. Referrals are made based on factual evidence. Whilst this can be in the form of observations from other professionals working with families and families themselves, providing a diary of times where behaviours occurred for example is a neat and factual way to get your concerns across. You could look at standard developmental milestones where your child is not typically developing, particularly surrounding communication and interaction with others, as well as any sensory challenges or sleep issues. Having provided these pieces of information in your first appointment, then of course describe the emotional effect on your child and your whole family. Emotional evidence is important and can get you access to a variety of support services. If you wish to be considered for an autism assessment though, have your factual evidence clear and ready. When I asked to be considered for an ADHD assessment, I took seven A4 pages of incidents, events and examples of behaviour with me. Practitioners are not mind readers, and they have to provide their reasons for referring patients. It's up to us to provide them with that evidence.

There are several possible outcomes to this initial appointment. Your

1   Cookman, 2018

child may be referred for an assessment, your child may be turned down for an assessment, you may be told to monitor your child and return if there is no change, or you may be referred for an assessment for a condition other than autism (there are several conditions that share similar presentations). Whatever the outcome, it will need some processing. If the outcome is not what you wanted then you are always able to ask for a second opinion.

If your child is referred for a diagnosis, this often means another long wait, which can be very distressing for your child, close family and friends. The wait can make you feel helpless, but there are lots of positive ways you can use this time. If your child is demonstrating traits of autism then a lot of the help you can offer them at home will be the same with or without a diagnosis. At this point you should educate yourself as much as possible about positive ways to mitigate some of the difficulties experienced by your child. It can be helpful to discuss their forthcoming assessment, if you haven't already, with family, friends and school staff. This will enable them to offer you support as well as to understand some of your child's actions and responses. School support should be based on need rather than a diagnosis so if your child's school is withholding support until you have a diagnosis, we would recommend a meeting with senior staff to discuss why this is.

What if I don't want my child assessed?

Some of you reading this may have been told that your child should be assessed for autism, or you may have a feeling that they are demonstrating autistic traits, but you may not want them to be assessed. If this is the case that is absolutely your choice and right to make that decision. Our only proviso would be to ask you ensure you have considered the impact that this decision has on your child and that you are making it with them at the heart of it.

There will be innumerable reasons why a parent may not want their child assessed for autism, and it is not our job to influence you either way. It is also worth saying that as there is no cure for autism, if your child is showing autistic traits there are things that you are able to do to support them without having to undergo an official assessment. As autism is a lifelong condition there is no limit on when they can be assessed for autism, and this may be something that you wish to discuss with your child when they are old enough to be involved in the decision to undergo assessment.

Preparing for the outcome of the assessment

If you have had a battle to get your child assessed, you will most likely be so relieved that you got the assessment that you won't necessarily have prepared yourself or your child for the outcome. Make sure that you give yourself time to consider how you will cope with various possible conclusions. What you say to your child will depend upon their age and understanding. Once again it is important to remember that there are no right or wrong ways to feel about a diagnosis. Feelings and emotions are reactions in the brain that you cannot control. What you *can* control is how you act. Be mindful of this: your child doesn't need to see their parent in floods of tears and terrified for their future (especially when you don't need to be). Give yourself time in private to process your emotions and you will soon realize how autism doesn't need to hold your child back in life. With the right support, they can achieve incredible things. Charlotte and I never thought we would be able to write this book, but no diagnosis was ever going to stop us. It's who we are, and we are proud of it.

An unexpected diagnosis

Occasionally, at the end of an assessment the outcome will be not to diagnose autism but another condition. This may come as major shock to parents and carers. If this does happen make sure that you ask the diagnosing clinician to signpost you to where you are able to get information. Whilst the outcome of Pie's autism assessment was expected, Charlotte has had other assessments with unexpected outcomes. The most recent example was when he was diagnosed with acquired brain injuries earlier this year. This was a complete shock because previously she had been told that his brain scans were normal. In fact they were showing no change to the initial one that showed the abnormalities, but she had not been told about them originally. With this diagnosis came a sense of relief that there were finally answers to Pie's difficulties, but at the same time a sense of grief that this diagnosis had taken so long and that opportunities to help him had been missed. Charlotte also experienced the feeling that she was totally unprepared for parenting a child with this diagnosis. After the initial shock she realized that she *did* know how to parent Pie and that his diagnosis was irrelevant to how she supported him. Charlotte did however read and learn as much as she could in order to understand fully why things happen and how best to support him.

CHAPTER RECAP

- An assessment does not always lead to a diagnosis of autism.
- Explore fully what an autism assessment entails so you can support your child.
- When asking a professional for a referral for an assessment, make sure you take enough evidence of why you believe your child is autistic.
- Be prepared for a different diagnosis to come out of the assessment.
- Consider the pros and cons of getting an assessment.

CHAPTER 5

SENSORY PROCESSING

Atypical sensory processing is an integral part of the presentation of autism and is something that is investigated as part of the autism diagnostic assessment. For some, sensory processing is looked at separately from the person's autism, but this is dependent upon geographic and diagnostic protocol rather than the level of sensory impairment. This is important to mention because whether or not your child has a sensory disorder diagnosed, if they are autistic then they will have challenges linked to their sensory processing. There are three broad areas of sensory processing irregularity, all with their individual features, and it is possible for a person to have more than one area of disturbance.

Irregularities with sensory modulation
The most recognized area is to do with the modulation of how the brain processes sensory input and output. A typical brain can control how it is affected by various sensory inputs. This is a natural, automatic process that the brain does without additional effort. However, in the autistic brain this encoding of sensory stimuli is not automatic, and whilst some learn coping strategies, there is no guarantee of accuracy, meaning that the person will always be potentially moments away from having to deal with a sensory crisis. One of the reasons why it is so hard to accurately learn how to modulate or control your brain's sensory levels and to support your child in their sensory development is that on occasion you can have a hyper or hypo response to the same stimuli.

One of the most noticed sensory irregularities parents discover early on is the way that their child processes pain, and this can also cause potential complications. One occasion that sticks in Charlotte's mind is when Pie was approximately five years old. She received a call from his school to say that he was very distressed, but nobody could understand why as there was no outward sign of illness or injury. When Charlotte arrived he was screaming and inconsolable. She managed to get him home and after three hours she noticed a tiny papercut on his finger. She put a plaster on and within half an hour it was as if nothing had been wrong. A couple of weeks later, Pie was admitted to hospital with sepsis; he had gone from appearing perfectly healthy showing no signs of discomfort or illness to full-blown sepsis requiring emergency treatment. Once he was in the high dependency unit, the doctor discovered he had ulcerated tonsilitis, which they estimated would have developed over at least four days and would have caused a great deal of pain. These two events demonstrate the different ways that his brain processed the sensation of pain.

Irregularities with sensory modulation can also create emotional responses and meltdowns, which can be perceived to be a behavioural response. Sensory-processing modulation challenges can cause distress, anxiety and at times aggression. Depending upon how a person's brain is regulating at any given time or in any given situation, it will also impact on whether they are seeking sensory input or avoiding it.

Sensory-based motor disorder

This is primarily concerned with the proprioception sense and has a great deal to do with a person's core stability and balance. These challenges are not experienced by every autistic person and are less common than sensory modulation challenges. If a person has postural differences then this can impact upon their balance and ability to learn movement patterns. The other way in which motor skills are impacted by sensory processing is with how we plan movement and the amount of pressure or force we use when doing something. This can cause problems with dressing, writing, using scissors and walking in crowded or cramped spaces where more precise motor planning is required.

Sensory discrimination disorder

The final area of sensory processing irregularity falls under the umbrella of sensory discrimination disorder. It can impact upon all the senses or a selection of them. Whichever sense is impacted, sensory discrimination disorder relates to the way that the brain is able to interpret information. One of Pie's biggest daily struggles is linked to auditory discrimination disorder. He will often mishear words that sound similar, for example "pat" and "cat". This means that there are delays in processing oral instructions and frequently a misunderstanding of what is being said. In turn this then impacts on self-esteem and confidence and leads to anxiety.

Your child's sensory profile

Now we have explained how sensory processing can impact upon an autistic person it is time to give some advice from our own personal experiences and those of Kiddo and Pie.

Children are often told "not to be so silly" or "you're just being fussy" due to them finding a taste, smell or sound painful or overwhelming. This can be extremely detrimental to a child's self-esteem. Constantly being told they don't feel or experience something in the way they do makes them doubt their own mind and whether or not their own feelings and experiences are valid in this world. It can lead to a child withdrawing and suffering in silence even though the pain they may be experiencing is very real. It also means their needs get ignored. So the first point to take from this chapter is that listening to how your child experiences the world around them is vital in helping them succeed and enjoy life.

In order to support your child and ensure their environment is one where they can relax, learn and sleep, you will need to work out what their sensory profile is. A sensory profile is a tool created from measuring and observing a person's reactions to different stimuli and environments. It identifies hyper sensitivities, hypo sensitivities, sensory patterns that might occur and most of all how these sensitivities cause barriers to learning, socializing and enjoying life. These profiles can be created by specialist professionals or informally by parents observing their child.

A sensory assessment isn't a one-size-fits-all assessment and there are a variety of assessments used dependent upon the developmental and chronological age of the patient. Some are mainly questionnaires completed by parents/carers and the observations of an occupational therapist whilst others are more in depth and practical. Pie has had several sensory assessments with varying outcomes. Most recently he had one that was specifically for people with intellectual disabilities, and this was by far the most useful and relevant assessment for him and provided some valuable information for everyone involved in his care.

During a sensory assessment the clinician will evaluate the individual's responses to everyday situations, chart the areas that need support and give advice on how to assist in supporting heightened sensory responses. Sadly these assessments are not always available in every area and you may find you need to research different senses in detail to learn about the specific needs of your child. By learning these things you can help keep your child much happier and find ways to support them if they're struggling with something many people find very simple.

As a teenager, I used to struggle with the smells when on a bus. I have an extremely hyper sensitive sense of smell and it causes me no end of problems, especially when I am out and about in public spaces. It was Charlotte who actually suggested that I use a little eucalyptus above my top lip and under my nose so that was all I could smell. It blocked out smells not only when I was out in public, but also if my husband was cooking a food I struggled with the smell of. Such a tiny adjustment made the world of difference to me.

Charlotte and I are not qualified occupational therapists (OTs), so this book does not include any questionnaires or resources for deciphering a sensory profile. However, we are able to explain how our sensory-processing differences impact upon our lives and what we have been able to do to help our sons. Additionally, we can recommend *The Out-of-Sync Child* by Carol Stock Kranowitz in particular, due to the questionnaires it has, the in-depth variety of sensory profiles and the number of games and ideas for each profile that promote sensory regulation.[1]

Sensory avoiders and sensory seekers

Two common terms used are "sensory avoider" and "sensory seeker". Avoiders are people who are hyper sensitive to stimuli and feel everything so deeply that it causes them actual pain. This causes them to avoid everyday activities that many would never believe could be associated with pain. For example, they may cover their ears when hearing any noise or always want to be sitting in a dark room because the sunlight is too bright for them. They may refuse baths and messy hands or complain that their shoes are uncomfortable. Often these people are known for being "fusspots" or "overly sensitive" and are told to toughen up and get on with it. These problems, however, cause very real pain for the person experiencing them. It is not a behavioural issue but a result of structural and chemical differences in the brain. Everyday life becomes too overwhelming and without the support they need they become withdrawn, refusing to leave the house as the outside world is too painful.

Sensory seekers are the opposite. They are hypo sensitive to stimuli, which means they don't get enough input from the outside world. They

---

1   Stock Kranowitz, 2005

seek out sensory experiences to feed their brain the information it is craving. These people love physical activity, multiple sensory experiences and a highly stimulating environment. Lights, sound, colour and movement: you name it, they want it. Often people with this profile may be termed as hyper or badly behaved.

When we first received a visit from an occupational therapist in relation to Kiddo they immediately said, "Oh, he is such a seeker, isn't he!" I thought this was odd for several reasons. First, they had only been watching him for five minutes, which was hardly reflective of his day-to-day behaviour. Second, I had witnessed a lot of avoidant behaviour particularly in regard to sound and light. Third, he hated people so spent most of the time trying to hide from this person. Now I actually liked our first OT. She did listen and she went through a thorough questionnaire on Kiddo's sensory type. However there seemed to be this determination to class him as either a seeker or an avoider. I was told that he was a sensory seeker and that we must help him experience as much physical activity as possible. Soft play, trampolines, swings, slides, the lot. Every day if possible. Initially this did make sense as Kiddo adored all these activities and so pretty much every day we were out trying to find him these physical activities. No matter how much of these activities he did though, he was never calm and satisfied by the end of it. In fact, the most usual pattern we fell into was taking a very excited two-year-old to soft play where he ran around like a mad man for the first 20 minutes and after that stopped responding to our parenting, became angry and eventually ended up in meltdown. I couldn't understand it; I was doing exactly what we had been told to do. That's when I bought *The Out-of-Sync Child* and quickly realized a very important fact.

People can be both sensory seekers *and* sensory avoiders. Whilst the assessment our local authority occupational therapist had undertaken did highlight some useful facts about Kiddo, I soon realized that it was a basic test to see whether he was predominantly a seeker or avoider. For many people this works brilliantly, but unfortunately Kiddo was way more complex than this and didn't fit neatly into either category. He was in fact both a seeker and an avoider, and his sensory needs changed daily or during the course of the same day. This meant that some days some things would be a problem and then other days they wouldn't. We had to learn how to both judge what his needs were that day, morning or afternoon, and also be prepared for them to change at any moment. Kiddo's sensory needs were and still are completely fluid, not fully fitting into either the sensory seeker or avoider category.

When he was three we decided that we would visit a private OT in London. He spent an entire morning with Kiddo in a room full of different sensory equipment. We filled in pages and pages of questionnaires and assessments. At the end of the assessment he called us in and there in the middle of the room was Kiddo lying on a flat, hard platform suspended in mid air with his hands hanging down loosely with the OT giving him a deep pressure massage. There was our boy, calm and regulated for what seemed like the first time since he was born. It was clear that his sensory needs were extremely complex and the report that followed confirmed this. Helping Kiddo to remain calm wasn't about giving him *all* of the sensory-seeking input we could. Neither was it about helping him avoid *all* of the input we could. It was a complete mix of both, and it changed every day, several times a day. Having had a year of complete carnage and meltdowns, I felt quite overwhelmed by this prospect. It took time but by keeping a diary of activities, the mood Kiddo woke up in and how his mood changed throughout the day, we eventually managed how to work out what he needed to keep him in the "regulation zone". The diary I used was a simple note-taking exercise. It noted when his moods changed, what his moods were, what activity we were doing at the time and the activities before and after so that we could see if there was any pattern to his trigger. Don't forget it is just as important to note the positive and happy moods as it is the negative ones.

The difference between the first OT we saw and the one we paid to go and visit privately was that the latter was a specialist in sensory integration therapy. Sensory integration therapy is still being researched but aims to help the person respond in a more organized way to stimuli. Basically, it helps them become calmer around overwhelming things. This is not a therapy that changes behaviour (remember, sensory processing is about the chemicals and structure in the brain); however, it may help an individual cope with processing light better over time, or deal with loud noises perhaps. This is not a service that is offered on the NHS in the UK. The NHS will assess people for difficulties and offer some recommendations for sensory tools or activities, but what it does not have the capacity for is to give each and every person continual therapy. Those resources are reserved for profoundly disabled individuals.

Keeping in the regulation zone

We left the assessment with a clear idea that our child adored some input and hated other input. It changed daily. So how did we learn how to keep our child within the "zone of regulation"? The following figure shows what we mean by the "zone of regulation".

Understimulated   Overstimulated

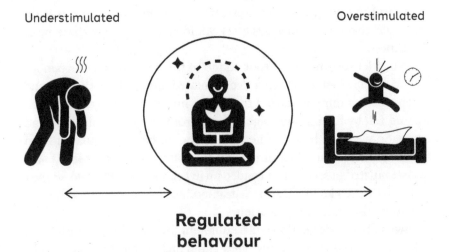

Regulated behaviour

As people with autism and/or ADHD, we are far more sensitive to changes in energy, weather, activities and routine. We adapt a sensory diet (activities to help keep us balanced) to fit round these things so that we can remain regulated and enjoy life. But what happens when major changes occur, and we don't adapt our sensory diet? Let's use the worldwide Coronavirus lockdowns as an example.

We all have a baseline, or "zone of regulation" as we like to call it. Most of us do things, whether subconsciously or consciously, to keep ourselves or our children in this zone so we are happy and regulated. For example, during term time perhaps your child comes home and is overstimulated so needs quiet time in a dark room. On the weekends they're understimulated so you do more physical activities like bouncing on the trampoline. In the school holidays this naturally changes because there is no school. Enter lockdown.

This hit my stimulation level like I have never known. I was completely understimulated. Because I couldn't do my usual routine I was laid out on the sofa unable to do anything. It was hell, and I needed a dopamine hit. So, I reached for my phone and started playing games and talking to people online. This lifted me into the regulation zone. Hooray it worked!

When the world started to open up, I found being on my phone too much made me feel tired, sluggish and bored. I was understimulated. But how? Because I was able to go out and do other things. I didn't need my phone any more in that way. What I hadn't done was to evaluate where I was at on my "stimulation scale".

As in the figure, I needed to stop and ask myself where I was on that scale, then judge what activities would help keep me in the zone of regulation.

When lockdown eased I took Kiddo to the park and on an open-air tram ride. He *loved* it! He remained regulated until right at the very end where the excitement started to tip him into overstimulation, which I could tell by his physical signs of eyes rolling back in his head and so on. So we went home. When we got home he was regulated from the car journey. Then I let him go on the trampoline. Disaster. He was overstimulated in seconds and ended up in full-blown meltdown for over an hour. Before I let him go on the trampoline I hadn't considered where he was on the scale of stimulation.

Signs of overstimulation will be different for each child. Some will be subtle and others very obvious. They could include giggling excessively, jumping, hand flapping, verbal stimming, the sudden inability to talk, anger or violent outbursts. It really is different for each child.

We are often told by OTs whether our children are sensory seekers or avoiders and told to make sure they get lots of the input they need. But what happens when the environment changes? Our baseline changes and we need different things. If we don't check in with ourselves and carry on with the same sensory diet we will, for want of a better phrase, be all over the place. Remember to take stock of where you are before deciding on activities. Maybe even get your kids to score from 1 to 10, 1 being bored and 10 being excited. It just might level out everyone's moods a little bit.

Sensory overload

So, what happens when you go too far one way and end up in a sensory overload meltdown? Charlotte has experienced this all her life, so for this next part of the chapter I will hand you over to her:

"Sensory overload is something I experience every day of my life, although it wasn't until about ten years ago that I actually realized that the way I felt was due to sensory overload and wasn't something that everyone experienced. When Pie was about three a consultant was busy talking about areas that he struggles with and one of her questions was 'Does he react abnormally to hand driers?' My response was no, as Pie responded to them the same way as I did. They obviously caused him pain and he had to get away from them as soon as possible. He demonstrated his dislike for hand driers by putting his hands over his ears and kicking his legs against the edge of his wheelchair. To me this was normal. Understanding Pie's sensory profile has actually been a cathartic experience for me and has taught me how to make changes to improve my life too.

Describing sensory overload is difficult because every overload feels completely different and is dependent upon so many factors. One of my first memories of a sensory overload was at my nursery school's harvest festival. We had all learnt about harvest, creating artwork, learning to sing a song and poem as well as bringing our harvest gifts. Given that this was all a large change from the normal routine of nursery I was looking forward to it, until I arrived at the church hall where my nursery took place. My grandmother opened the door and immediately I wanted to run: the noise of the parents and grandparents talking, the chairs being moved loudly along the floor, the other children happily playing – it felt as if it was all being whirled around my head with different sounds taking over my auditory system at various times and volumes. At the same time I felt sick because of the combination of new smells: the flowers, vegetables, fruits and all the adults, many of whom I now assume were wearing perfume, which was overwhelming my olfactory system. The battle of these two sensory systems were causing such turmoil that I was sick and then let out the loudest of screams. This resulted in an abrupt end to all the noises that were causing so many problems in my head; my scream was louder than them all and it helped to regulate them because I could focus on the noise I was making instead of the noises made by others, which I could neither control nor process.

For me, not all sensory overloads happen in busy places; they can happen when I am within the security of my own home and on my own with no seemingly obvious sensory stimuli. I have very acute hearing, especially when it comes to pitch and rhythm; often words in conversations can appear muffled and as if they are being delivered through a crackly gramophone speaker. Pitch and rhythm are always very clear to me and the musician in me is always trying to relate these noises to particular musical motifs or patterns. This may appear to be a quirky artistic response, but it is far more than that. It can become obsessive and eventually create a sensory overload when my brain is not able to cope with any more of the exact thing it was craving minutes before. Owing to my dyslexia I rely on auditory input a great deal. Words and phrases are processed initially through patterns and quite often if I am trying to remember a word or attempting to spell it I will eventually recall it by its rhythm. For me pitch and rhythm are not simply musical devices, they are present everywhere. If I am buying a computer, the sound of the keyboard keys is an essential factor for me! The noise of the central heating boiler warming up can come across as an industrial symphony with various clicks, vibrations and whirling, all creating a sensory feast. Most mornings in the winter I delight in the knowledge that I will be privy to my own morning serenade courtesy of the hot water and central heating. One November morning a few years ago I was waiting for the performance to begin when all of a sudden our dog Daisy started to snore. Daisy has a loud snore and I accept this; however on this occasion it was enough to turn my joyous start to the day into a meltdown. The lower register of Daisy's snore was discordant with the water tank and caused my ears physical pain. Thankfully Daisy remembered that the heating turning on is a sign that the day is about to begin and breakfast won't be far away. Despite this discordant start to the day only lasting a few minutes, the effects were longer lasting and I struggled to process anything for a number of hours and felt mentally drained for the rest of the day with my head replaying the noises that were so problematic to my brain.

Not all sensory overload can be attributed to a specific input. It is usually a combination of a variety of factors. This form of sensory overload will be similar to what most of your children will experience at school. Having taught in primary schools for over 12 years it is no surprise to me that so many children struggle when they get home. From my experience of this kind of sensory overload in myself, Pie and other children, I know it is made worse by the fact that the day will have been spent masking, which in itself puts a strain on the sensory system.

Some people will have a vision of schools as being places of order, routine and calmness. The reality is somewhat different as schools are noisy, full of disruption and a toxic mix of anxiety, excitement and mischief. The noise levels are often unbearable especially in a 1930s purpose-built school building with high ceilings and little insulation, allowing for the smallest of sounds to reverberate – suddenly a pencil being dropped sounds like a loud thunderclap. At Pie's school the acoustics in the main hall were amplified to such a degree that soundproofing was installed as part of his education, health and care (EHC) plan. There are also the weekly fire alarm checks, the half-termly whole-school fire practice and in some schools beeping fire doors that set off an irritating noise when they automatically close.

The lighting too can be problematic. Often large fluorescent lights have an irritating habit of developing intermittent flickers and buzzing.

This combines with the glare of large whiteboards, where the majority of a child's learning now occurs, and laptops. School windows have limited blinds so this can mean that there are times of the day when the sun gleams in with nothing anybody can do about it. These visual stimuli can not only cause pain and discomfort, but they also stop the child from learning or completing their work.

Next on my list is smell. Classrooms are smelly places. Large groups of children confined to small places with the added effects of a PE lesson on a hot day or digesting a lunch, fragranced stationery and from Year 5 upwards the obsession with spraying body sprays between lessons in an attempt to cover all existing aromas. Depending on the layout of the school building, there is for most of the day the smells from the school kitchens where several different dishes are often being prepared in large quantities.

Schools are a place where the sense of touch is also put through its paces. In a school day the child will have to be in contact with a variety of different stationery items – whiteboard, computers, books and paper – and will have to adapt at pace to the feel of these. There is then the potential for different clothing, for example PE kits, art overalls, lab coats and in the winter the putting on and taking off of outdoor clothing.

Finally, there is the onslaught on the proprioceptive system during the school day. Different seating in various areas of the school building from a cold floor to a plastic chair to a bean bag – whatever the person's preference their body is still having to process all of these different sensations. School corridors are often narrow and crowded, meaning that any form of motor planning is impossible, and you have people bumping into you. Playgrounds, whilst more spacious, still present many proprioceptive challenges with children noisily running around in different directions.

Not only are all of these experiences challenging, children also have to deal with numerous transitions in a school day between different teachers, learning areas, playgrounds and so on. For those children who may have additional support during the school day, this can result in additional transitions as they may have to access smaller learning clusters away from their main classroom base. Even within a classroom setting there are the regular interruptions of ancillary staff collecting a child for a medical appointment or passing on a message, or additional teachers in the classroom for observations.

When describing the effects of a school day on a person with autism, I use the analogy of a bottle of fizzy drink. Every time the person experiences a sensory challenge the bottle is shaken. When the child returns home the parent opens the bottle and the almost volcanic eruption is the sensory overload and/or meltdown, which the parent is left to deal with at the end of the school day."

It's so important to understand how someone with sensory processing disorder might feel. Charlotte explains it fantastically and gives you an idea of the pain and anguish it can cause in everyday living. By working out what your child is over- or understimulated from, you can support and ease this pain both at home and out in the world.

Observe your child

Without the input of a professional, learning about your child's profile really is down to observation. If you are able to ask them, talk to them about the things they find really difficult to tolerate, or the things they really enjoy that make them feel calm or awake. Whilst questionnaires are quick, they may not give you the full picture. Notes and experiences over a number of weeks or months are the best way to get the most accurate information, especially if your child isn't able to talk about how they feel. Whilst you may feel you need information quickly, persevering with this task will help you hugely in later years. Remember, some sensory differences will be hugely obvious, and you can use this information to create a safe space for your child at home where they can regulate. If they don't like light then make them a dark tent. If they spend lots of time looking at changing colours and lights then look for objects like lava lamps or fibre optic lamps where they can visually stim and regulate that way. Trial and error may be needed, and gentle and controlled exposure to different things at home will help you gauge your child's reaction to stimuli in the outside world.

Sensory toys

Having worked out what your child's sensory profile is, the next step most people take is to buy an abundance of sensory toys. Or, if you're like me, you heard your child might be autistic, you linked it to the word "sensory" and you bought every single sensory toy available, thinking your child needed it. As previously mentioned, we recommend *The Out-of-Sync Child* for working out sensory profiles and it will also recommend sensory toys that can help with each category of sensory processing. Here are a few hints and tips on where to buy your sensory stash:

- Be aware of sensory toy sites. These sites attach premium price tags to items that could be considered a medical help to people. Always double check that bargain sites or shops are not selling the same or similar item for a lot less. Exercise balls and peanut balls can be found for just a few pounds so make sure you're not spending over the odds.
- How much space have you got? Some sensory items are quite large. Make sure you have the space to keep them.
- Can your child use them safely without you? Some items require excellent balance or a safety judgement from your child. Can you leave it out or does it need to be locked away?
- Will/does your child become overwhelmed at having too many sensory toys in one place? How will you help them choose which activity or item is best for them that day?
- How will you know when your child has had enough sensory input? Will you use a timer? Watch for signs of regulation or dysregulation?

These are all things I didn't find out until years after Kiddo's sensory needs were looked at. I remember a visit from OT number three who said we needed to immediately remove the indoor trampoline so that Kiddo could only have access to it when he really needed it, otherwise he would be constantly overstimulating himself. Great advice that we immediately followed! It was just three years too late. The trampoline was promptly placed in the shed, where it stayed for some time. Kiddo didn't seem to need it any more, which we couldn't understand. Eventually we had a lightbulb moment where we realized that it was because he didn't need it *at home*. He wasn't understimulated at home; he was overstimulated because he had been at school all day. He wanted quiet and darkness at home. School however was a different story. His body would have excess energy from the ADHD but his brain would be slow and sluggish. He needed to stimulate his brain, use up some excess energy and land somewhere in the middle. So we sent the trampoline and several other items to his classroom for him to use throughout the day.

This has been transformational. Every item is now getting used as it is in the right environment for him. At home he has calming items inside and stimulating items outside for weekends and holidays. In his classroom he has a whole range of toys and we have worked with his teachers and learning disability nurse to decipher what piece works at the right time. Some days he will arrive at school overstimulated and so I will suggest to the staff which pieces of equipment he uses and which he stays away from that day. Every person is different, and each person will be affected by sensory equipment differently. It's your job to work out which ones are right for your child.

Sensory breaks

In the same way, each child will need different types of sensory breaks according to their sensory profile. In essence a sensory break is having a break from a sedentary activity such as sitting at a desk. For most children with autism these are scheduled into their school day as they enable sensory-seeking children the opportunity to regulate, which in turn enables them to focus more and engage with their learning. Sensory-avoidant children may need a break from the classroom and to sit and regulate in a quiet, dark area away from the noise of others. It is essential to remember that even if the child looks like they don't need a sensory break, they should be given it. This prevents the build-up of dysregulation throughout the day. A child may not even realize they need it until they are actually doing the sensory activities they have been given. It's about letting the steam escape before the pressure builds up and the child explodes.

It is important not to ignore this fantastic tool when at home. All too often for children who attend an education provision there is a tendency to accidentally compartmentalize home and school.

A sensory break is easy to implement and can range from jumping or skipping to playing with a fidget toy or having time on a swing. It is easy to plan a sensory break anywhere, and used in the right way they can often divert a meltdown or shutdown.

Before we bring this chapter to a close we want to list the mistakes we made when trying to help our children with their sensory needs. We have mentioned most of them already but just to be clear, here's a list of what *not* to do:

1. Do not assume your child fits neatly into the sensory seeker or avoider box. They can be both and their profile can change daily.
2. Do not buy hundreds of sensory toys without working out which one your child needs first. OTs often have access to sensory libraries where you can try equipment out for free.
3. Do not place sensory equipment where it isn't needed. Make sure your sensory equipment is situated in the right environment.

A piece of calming equipment is not going to help you regulate your child in an environment where they are already understimulated.

4. Do not forget to evaluate how your child is feeling before setting off for a sensory-filled activity. What will they need to regulate afterwards? When do they need to stop? When has the activity regulated them?

CHAPTER RECAP

- All autistic people have atypical sensory processing of some sort.
- Sensory dysregulation is often a major contributor to meltdowns.
- A person's sensory profile frequently evolves and changes.
- Sensory breaks are valuable for all people with autism. They are often timetabled into a child's school day but don't forget to use them at home.
- Not all sensory overloads can be attributed to a specific trigger.

CHAPTER 6

EDUCATION

When most parents think of education they envisage schools, exams and desks. But, as with all things when you are dealing with autistic children, you will need to open your mind to a different concept, and that is one of the few things that applies to all autistic children regardless of their presentation. This was one of the greatest challenges for Charlotte with Pie. As a teacher herself, and as an autistic person who had a relatively positive school experience, it was one of those moments when she realized it was time to adapt her thought process, and you will have to as well.

Education and learning are not all about academic success. Depending upon your child's presentation, their childhood education may be preparing them for a top university or to learn to be able to order a drink in a cafe or use a washing machine and everything in between. This doesn't matter. What is important is that your child has an education experience that is appropriate to their needs, that is engaging and that provides them with the tools that they will need to fulfil their potential as an autistic adult. Where this happens, who provides it and what exams they pass are not the main factors.

Finding the right education placement

Finding the right education for your child is one of the hurdles that all parents have to overcome, but there may be a few more turbulent periods along the way when finding the best provision for your autistic child. Hopefully we shall be able to give you some general guidance, and the chapter ends with three individual stories of the education journeys of autistic children.

First, we will look at schools as this is where most children begin their journey in formal education. In the UK there are three main options when it comes to schools: mainstream, specialist hubs and specialist schools. The majority of autistic children will attend mainstream schools and whilst they may require additional support or adaptations, they will be able to access the education provided alongside their neurotypical peers.

Some mainstream schools have units or hubs attached to them. These are often in different parts of the building or sometimes a separate building altogether but within the school grounds. These all operate in unique ways but there are often times when the children will work within the mainstream school and other times will work within the hub when more support is needed, or a holistic or therapeutic method is required.

Finally, there are specialist provisions. These provide for several presentations, covering all disabilities and medical conditions. The specialist provisions designed for autistic children range from schools where the children will learn an age-appropriate curriculum, which may be delivered in a differentiated fashion and in smaller classes, to schools for autistic children and those with profound learning needs.

Without a doubt there is a growing understanding that school is not for everyone and there are more and more schools available that are offering forest learning or specific skill-based learning, such as farm or land studies. It is sometimes possible to agree with your child's school that a flexible curriculum may suit them best, so they access a traditional school provision for part of the week and the rest of the time they attend another school.

The final option is home education, which in the UK falls into two categories: elective home education and Education Other Than at School (EOTAS). The first is when a parent chooses to remove their child from a school, or decides never to enrol them in school, and takes on responsibility for educating their child on their own. The second is when it is decided that school is not an option for a child either because no suitable school can be found or because the child's needs are too complex or high need to be provided by a school.

When deciding upon the correct provision for your child it is important that you are aware of the legal regulations in your country surrounding the education of children with additional needs. In England and Wales this is stated in the special educational needs and disability (SEND) code of practice, which exists to clarify the support a child or young person with additional needs is entitled to, which is upheld in law. If you are thinking about a less traditional educational approach for your child, then once again check the legal status of this in your country to make sure that you are working within the legal framework.

Looking at how to find the correct school provision for your child is a minefield. As we have already said most autistic children will receive their education in a mainstream school and even more will begin their school journey in a mainstream setting, especially if they do not have a co-existing diagnosis of a learning disability. This doesn't mean however that they will not need or not be entitled to additional help and support. To find out what this is and how it relates to your child you will need to refer to what is offered locally. However, there is broad parity internationally so we shall refer to the English system from now on as this is what we are familiar with and what Charlotte has experienced as an autistic child, parent and teacher.

The timing of your child's diagnosis

We are going to look at three examples of finding the right school for your child based on three different profiles and situations. The first is for a child who has a diagnosis of autism before they start their formal education, but it has been decided that their needs will be supported in a mainstream school and they don't have any legally enforceable support plans.

In this scenario you will most likely be looking at schools in your local area. Ensure that you visit as many schools as possible and when you visit, be honest with the school about your child's diagnosis and how it impacts upon their social development and sensory processing as well as their learning. Ask if they have other pupils who have an autism diagnosis and ask for examples of how they have been supported and provided with a differentiated education. This may not always be relevant to your child, but it is a good marker of how supportive a school is and what their understanding of autism is.

When you visit look at class sizes and the configuration of classrooms. It might be that a school in a village has ten pupils per class, but if they have cramped classrooms and learning environments then it might not be beneficial to an autistic pupil, compared to a school with classes of 30 children but who have larger classrooms and more quiet spaces to access.

When you visit a school, especially if it is as part of a wider open day, it might be difficult to get a genuine feel of the school. For this reason we would suggest seeing if you can talk to parents who have an autistic child at the school. You can hear about their experiences and also read the school's latest inspection report, paying particular attention to any reference of how they support pupils with additional needs.

Second, there will be children who are already attending school when they have their assessment for autism and diagnosis. It may be that they masked most of their symptoms in their preschool years, but their traits became more evident once they started school. It is important to remember that if your child is making progress at school and is settled and happy then a diagnosis of autism doesn't have to mean a change of provision. In this scenario it could be potentially damaging to do so as too many changes for no reason may cause the child significant stress. Sometimes following a diagnosis a child may receive one-to-one support in their current school for all or part of their school day.

Third, if your child was assessed for autism as part of a wider quest for an appropriate provision, or as part of an education support plan, then looking for a new school will be necessary. You will hopefully have received guidance from professionals working with you as to which schools may be suitable for your child. If you haven't then ask or look for local parenting support charities that offer advice on education. Once you have the names of some potentially suitable schools then visit them and follow the guidance already given. If your child will be attending a specialist school, it is important to remember that these are not always local. When considering the suitability of these schools don't forget to consider how a journey will impact upon the child, whether it fits around any siblings and so on, whether transport will be provided, or the cost covered by your local authority.

Some parents will be in the same situation as Charlotte and me: knowing that their child's needs will not be able to be met in a mainstream setting. They will already have an official education support plan (EHC plan in England) or be in the final stages of getting one. There are pros and cons to being in this situation. On the one hand your search for a provision is more structured, and you will have most likely got a detailed formal assessment that clearly states what your child needs from an education setting. On the other hand, you might have more restrictions on schools that will offer your child a place. However, if your child needs this specialist support your overall feeling will be one of relief that you have managed to get your child's needs acknowledged by the correct professionals so early on in their journey.

Specialist schools

The basic principles surrounding the selection of a specialist school are the same as for a mainstream one, although there may be different regulations around visiting any prospective schools. These restrictions on visiting will be done to reduce the impact on their current pupils, so whilst they may seem frustrating additions to an already stressful process, it shows that the school puts the needs of their pupils first.

Specialist schools have clearly defined entry criteria in England. These are based not only on the child's diagnoses and presentation but also whether the child has an EHC plan. Before looking at any schools make sure that your child meets both criteria.

Regardless of the sort of provision your child is going to attend, if you do not get the school of your choice and you feel that there is a very valid reason why your child should attend that school, parents always have a right to appeal. This can be a draining process but one that is frequently necessary. If you decide to embark on an appeal, consider the following points:

- Have you got a valid reason for your appeal? If your child is a wheelchair user and you have been offered a school on multiple levels with limited access, then yes, you do, but if you want them to go to a specific school because a friend from nursery goes there then this argument is not likely to hold up in court.
- Is the alternative definitely not suitable? Always double check; sometimes it might be a school you had not thought of considering or one that you had discounted. Do your research again, and if possible have a repeat visit to be 100 per cent certain.
- Have you got the appropriate support and/or knowledge to embark on an appeal or tribunal? You don't need to have a legal representative so it doesn't come down to money, but look for local charities that may be able to help you with your appeal.
- Finally, and most importantly, is it in your child's best interest to appeal? I don't mean only about the school place, but if they are going to have a stressed and exhausted primary carer that might not be in their best interests if the first two points in this list cannot be fully justified.

Preparing your child for school

Once you have the school place sorted out it is then about preparing your child. They may need to get used to wearing a uniform; it might be helpful to walk near the school a few times so that they can get used to what it looks like. If starting school will mean a routine change at home then it is best to introduce these changes gradually, so that your child is given time to adapt and adjust rather than having to add that to their processing when their first day at school arrives. All of these things are a normal part of preparing any child for the start of their formal education. However, it is essential – even if you are anxious about how they will cope (which is perfectly normal) – that you don't let your child pick up on your anxieties. When talking about school use simple, positive language and choose your words carefully to make sure that you are not reinforcing your child's fears. At the same time, they will need time to be able to talk about their own feelings and how starting school is making them feel. This open dialogue, whether verbal, through colouring, through play or through any other means of communication, will be key to being able to support your child through their schooling, and there is no better time to lay the foundations for that than right now.

Every school will induct their new pupils and parents according to their own individual process. It is important though that you are given an opportunity to explain to your child's teacher and SEN coordinator about your child. Sometimes a letter is a good way to do this as it will go on their file and will mean that it can be referred back to as and when necessary. This doesn't have to be very long or all about what your child can't do. A balanced introduction to your child by the person who knows them best is what you need to aim for. Important things to cover include what they like doing, what calms them, any known triggers and whether or not they mask their emotions. There is nothing worse than teachers reporting that your child was fine in school when you are trying to find out why most evenings result in a meltdown. If you explain to the teacher early on about their masking you will be able to refer them back to that if this does happen.

Continuing this open dialogue throughout your child's education is crucial. Let the school know when things work, when they don't work and if you are noticing changes to your child's presentation that may need support in school. It is important to keep communication balanced and not only negative. Make sure you remember to communicate the things that are going well, in order to ensure that an open and honest relationship develops between home and school.

As we have already mentioned, once your child starts school there will be a routine change. Some autistic children will need a completely static routine to start with so they are not thrown by any changes. Others may need familiarity at certain key points in the morning, but the remainder of the time they are able to have a more flexible approach. For some, having cues to the morning routine is helpful as are timetables that cover both home and school life. It is important though to remember that not all autistic children need this or want it. Whilst Kiddo sometimes benefits from routine charts, now and next boards and timetables, for Pie they cause a great deal of anxiety and overwhelm as he can't process it all. Once again, do what is right for your child. This will probably be through trial and error, and it may not always remain the same. If your child has used visual timetables but then appears to not benefit from them, take them away and vice versa.

The same can be said for transitions. The transition between home and school and back again is exhausting for autistic children. You will find out what works for your child, and you will find some ideas that you can apply to this transition in the chapters on going out and play. It doesn't matter what ingredients make up your transition, but the end product needs to be a transition that is as calm, happy and relaxed as possible with the supporting adults knowing what is required of them in order for this to be facilitated. There will be transitions throughout the school day, and if you have a process that works for your child to deal with transition then make sure the school are aware of this.

Whilst the transition from school to home will for most children be less stressful than the one from home to school, never underestimate the impact of any transition for an autistic person. The major difference following the school to home transition is that your child will be having to process their school day and regulate their senses. It is important to allow your child the time and the tools to do this. It might be alone time, screen time, a favourite snack, an opportunity to talk to you or the opportunity to play with their favourite toy. This time will be key to giving your child the best possible afterschool experience.

For older children, and especially those in mainstream schools, there will be an expectation that they will do homework. Some children will find this a welcome opportunity for them to cover some of the things they learnt in school whilst in a more familiar and less stressful environment. It can also mean they have more time to complete work and are not pressured by lesson times. It can however be a concept that is met with a great deal of refusal. This isn't necessarily a sign of laziness or lack of interest in their education; it can be the rigidity in their thought process that schoolwork happens at school. It might be worth discussing with the school to see if they can attend a homework club after school or if the school can agree to a reduction in homework or an understanding if it is not completed on time or even not at all.

Naomi's story

As you are aware by now, every autistic person us unique, and this applies to how they cope with school. However, there are some key challenges that are faced by most autistic children throughout their school years. Naomi has kindly shared with us her personal experiences of what it is like for her as an autistic child attending a mainstream primary school:

Morning preparation – I wake up and come downstairs and try not to think about school too much. I get my iPad or toys and set them up just how I like it. I know I need to get dressed and eat but until things are "right" I can't think about those things. I need to do one thing at a time so please leave me alone. Let me do it my way. Constantly asking me questions is so stressful, as is nagging me about time. By the time we need to leave I am already stressed and anxious.

In the playground – I am scanning. This is so hard to see who I need to see when everyone is dressed the same and moving around. The noise, the unpredictable movements, the bags on the ground... that's a lot to take in for me. I only want to find my best friend and the longer it takes to find her the more I get worried. What if she is off sick? What if she has an appointment today?

Getting to class – I have to remember to put my bag one place, my packed lunch somewhere else and then hang my coat on the right peg. It can be confusing to remember all that while others are talking and moving all around me, and the lights are so bright inside. Sometimes I wait until most of the others are in the class but then I worry I will get shouted at for taking too long! Sometimes I forget I have my school bag as it is on my back and I can't see it! How can everyone else do this so quickly and easily and I can't?

Class – I listen so much. In fact I listen so hard to everything that sometimes I can't do my work because I need to stop and listen to everything the teacher says in case she is talking to me. I want to write neat because I don't want a row but then they say I need to work faster and I can't do fast and neat. It is hard to concentrate with others so close to me. They move about and talk and turn pages and it is so distracting sometimes. The walls have so much stuff on them, I can hear the tap dripping and I can hear people walking about.

I am scared to talk in case I get in trouble – Sometimes I just can't do the work. Yesterday they wanted us to do a senses poem about fireworks. They told me to imagine being at a bonfire with fireworks but how can you do that if you have never been to a bonfire before? I haven't. They told me to write about what I would touch but you are not allowed to touch fireworks so I can't write anything. They told me to write what I can smell but all I can smell right now is disgusting school dinners and I can't even spell that. I just leave that one too. Then the teacher gets me in trouble for not doing the task. I want to cry. The tears won't come out.

Playtime – I don't understand this bit. You play with toys so why call it playtime when there are no toys? Just call it "talk time" or "stand in the playground time" instead. I take my own toys out. Then it rains and we have to come inside and I can't play with my toys and it is so confusing for me. I don't like changing things. I get cold at playtime because it is hard to fasten my coat and if I take my time then people tell me to hurry up and go outside so I just can't fasten it up now. I have one area I like to stand and play with my one friend. We play the same game every day. We like it that way. I want to play with others but I can't because I don't understand what they are playing. They don't have toys. I can't work out made-up games like that.

Lunchtime – Lunchtime is horrible. We have a short time for every-one in the whole school to eat and they want us all to line up and take turns and sit at huge tables with other children I don't know. I just want to sit down and get time to eat and not have to hear chatter and smell what everyone else has that I don't like. It is far too noisy and busy and yet no one will open my yoghurt or peel my banana. I feel lost and confused and just want out of there.

PE – I hate PE so much. I never know what we are going to do. Sometimes we do balls and sometimes running and sometimes sports. I hate it all. I know I can't do it and people laugh. How can I catch a ball when there is so much else going on in the same hall at the same time? I can't focus. I am so cold. My legs don't like not having trousers on. My arms miss my cardigan so much. I once fell and hurt myself in PE so I don't run now because running is dangerous, plus they said at assembly to not run in school so I don't run. Then they tell me to run and I want to ask "but you said not to run in school" but my voice won't work. I want to cry. The tears won't come.

After school – I do like school. I like learning and I like doing work. I like having a desk and I really want to be star of the week. I like the other children though I don't know if they like me. I want to tell you about things that have bothered me, like being told to work quicker or not eating. I am tired from it all and now I feel safe. I want to cry. This time the tears will come so please let them. I am okay. I just need to let the day at school wash away so I can rest. School can be hard but then every day can sometimes be hard when you have autism like me.

Obviously not every autistic child will have these difficulties, but it hopefully gives you as a parent an idea of some of the challenges faced by your children when accessing schools. It doesn't mean that your child can't be happy in school or that they shouldn't be there, but it is a good explanation of what one autistic child experiences and will hopefully help you to understand why your child may struggle so much, especially after school.

"School refusal"

Autistic children in particular can, what we believe is wrongly, become known as school refusers. These children find school overwhelming to the point that they are unable to engage in the school-based education offered by their current placement. This may be a temporary state where the child needs the opportunity to have their needs understood so that reasonable adaptions can be made to ensure that they are able to access school. There will also be those who are traumatized by school to the extent that they are later diagnosed with post-traumatic stress disorder (PTSD).

School refusal is different to a child who may decide once or twice a year that they need time to regulate rather than go to school. It is important that if this is your child you don't panic that this one-off occurrence means they won't ever set foot in school again. Every child's reason for not being able to attend school – whether for a couple of days, months or years – will be different. It is essential that from the start parents have an open and honest dialogue with the school so that as a team you are able to look at ways to support your child in their education.

Home educating

There are those children who do not receive their education in school. In the UK you are legally allowed to elect to educate your child at home. If they are already in school, then you need to de-register them from school by writing a letter informing the school of your choice to home educate. This can't be done if your child is in a specialist provision without the placement being changed on their EHC plan. For some autistic children and their families this solution works very well, and they find that they can access learning better, tailor the learning to their child and have a greater freedom and choice when it comes to their child's education. I know first-hand that there are times when this route works brilliantly, but it isn't a decision to be rushed or taken lightly. If your child doesn't have a team of professionals working with them outside of school, then de-registration and subsequent elective home education can cause difficulties if or when you need specialist help and support for your child.

Another area of home education Charlotte has first-hand experience with is when your child is classed as receiving their education "other than at school". In this situation the local authority still has responsibility for supporting their education and if they have an EHC plan then this will be maintained by the local authority. Sometimes children who receive this provision are provided with tutors and input from the local authority whilst others receive a direct funding package that allows for a more tailormade approach and gives a greater choice of the professionals who work with the child.

Extracurricular activities

Wherever your child receives their education, remember that extracurricular activities should never be underestimated, as it isn't only about the skill your child learns at this activity but other benefits that are far more significant. Charlotte knows that she wouldn't have been able to achieve any of her formal qualifications if she had not had music. Music has always helped her to regulate, and as a child it gave her the confidence to perform, take examinations and learn to believe in herself. Music meant it didn't matter to Charlotte if she didn't have friends in the playground or if she didn't understand the latest trend. It also gave her a method of communication that didn't require words, which was a relief.

We have both ensured that our sons have their own interests and hobbies outside of their formal education. For Pie it is horse riding. He gets on a horse, and it doesn't matter that he finds walking difficult and painful or that he can't write. On a horse he is master of his own destiny and becomes both confident and happy.

For Kiddo it is swimming, and we are writing this just a couple of hours after I proudly sent Charlotte a photograph of the 50-metre swimming certificate he had just achieved aged seven! These experiences (and achievements) give our children essential life experiences and skills, which they may be able to transfer into other areas of their learning and their lives.

You may have felt that there has been a lack of specific advice in this chapter; that is mainly down to education being a personal choice, specific to the area you live in and what is offered in your country. We could have filled it with specific advice and legal entitlement but living 177 miles from each other we know that there are so many differences in what is available to our boys. With that in mind we thought it would be better for us to give you an insight into our boys' education journeys and what we have learnt from them.

Danielle's story

I knew Kiddo had needs that would go beyond what mainstream would offer, and when he was two I was told by a paediatrician to get him into my local mainstream provision at the earliest possible age. This was to ensure that the lengthy process of assessing his educational needs, which would eventually lead to the choice of his provision, could begin as early as possible and be in place before his formal school journey would begin at age five.

I made an appointment with my local school and met with the head-teacher to explain his needs. A huge concern of mine was his complete lack of awareness of any danger, and I requested a one-to-one staff member. Back then schools could apply to a fund for extra staffing in these situations. Nowadays that funding has ceased to exist in most places.

We agreed that I should bring Kiddo in twice a week after school for him to familiarize himself with the classroom environment and the staff.

His extensive needs were immediately highlighted. A one-to-one staff member was appointed, and he began attending shortly after he turned three. The school and I made several observations of his struggles and very soon it became clear that mainstream could not cater for his needs. His transition to specialist provision was quick and smooth. We are aware that this is not the case for so many families and often what leads to a lengthy transition is when parents and the school do not have aligned beliefs in what is best for the child.

Kiddo's school and I agreed on his needs and together took a proposal to our local authority for him to be moved. It was nothing other than pure luck that a preschool space was available, and he started specialist provision the following academic year, still age three.

Kiddo finds the transitions to and from school extremely difficult. However, once home in the afternoon he is usually very happy. There is no delayed reaction and no meltdown. He talks to himself and processes the day but he isn't distressed whilst doing this. To me this is a strong sign that school itself isn't the problem. I've seen photos and videos of him enjoying his work as well.

However, if you saw him when transitioning from me to a teacher, you would be forgiven for thinking he hated school. He doesn't. For one thing, he voluntarily gets in the car in the mornings with the right sensory distractions. If it was school that was a problem for him, nothing would help him leave the house at all.

Charlotte's story

Pie had a slightly different path and was fortunate that he had a statement of educational needs (the predecessor to an EHC plan) in place just after his second birthday, whilst still in hospital. At that time the outcomes for Pie were very unknown and I didn't want him to miss out on valuable opportunities if his difficulties were down to delay rather than a specific disorder. Pie attended a small, independent Montessori nursery from the age of three until five. The Montessori pedagogy is very autism friendly. It is a multi-sensory approach and children are given activities according to their stage, not chronological age. Pie started in the toddler room where his peers were 12–18 months old and he had a minimum of one-to-one support at all times. The nursery staff were exemplary in meeting his medical and developmental needs as well as allowing him to develop in his own unique and idiosyncratic way.

Every achievement, difficulty and observation was written down and when there was an area that needed more support they were quick to inform the local authority. Pie loved this setting so much that being a summer baby meant they had the flexibility to keep him in nursery rather than start primary school. During his final year at nursery, it was decided that Pie would attend the local specialist school for children with moderate learning difficulties, which also catered for children with complex medical needs.

This was a disaster from the outset. Pie was too complex for them. Also, because of his weakened immune system, he spent more time at home with infections or having to isolate if there was a case of chicken-pox or other childhood illness in the school meaning that there was no opportunity for him to get into a routine or benefit from the educational support on offer. They persisted for two years although Pie's attendance averaged at around 30 per cent. Following medical advice, they applied to de-register him which was agreed by the local authority, and Charlotte electively home educated him from Years 3 to 6.

Having the flexibility to adapt his learning to his level and his health, and to recap and repeat things as required, Pie made good relative progress. They also had two or three hospital appointments most weeks so his education could fit around this. Towards the end of Year 5 Charlotte knew that Pie's needs were becoming too complex and severe for her teaching skills and at his annual education review it was decided that they would look for a school-based provision. Pie's profile was by this point changing rapidly, which made a difficult task impossible. Following an exhaustive search, no school could be found, and the local authority provided tutors for 10 hours a week. This enabled Pie to transition his learning from Charlotte to another trusted adult, but progress was slow and his profile was not matching his diagnosis, which caused more problems for the tuition service who had been given several unrealistic attainment targets and their attendance became somewhat sporadic.

Following a further search for a school for Pie, they were then given a direct payment package enabling more flexibility and a greater holistic approach to his learning. He has had an amazing tutor for four years who adapts the curriculum in a way most teachers could only dream of. Who could have imagined that the Industrial Revolution could be taught using Play-Doh? Horse riding and time in the community with a personal assistant were also funded as well as therapies.

When Pie turned 16 it was decided that he didn't get much benefit from education, and he now has a package of day care. This includes life skills, activities, horse riding and spending time with a devoted team who share the aim of making Pie's life as happy and as fulfilled as possible.

This sentiment brings us nicely to the end of this chapter with some advice from Charlotte, who had quite set ideas of what education looked like. Who had a blinkered approach as to the importance of academia, who had to fight for the right support for 11 years and who was always worried that it wasn't right. But do you know – it was just what Pie needed, and at 16 Pie is a happy young man who has interests and hobbies and who enjoys his learning. These are his educational achievements, and Charlotte couldn't be prouder. After all, what do pages of qualifications tell us about a person?

CHAPTER RECAP

- Don't be afraid to look outside the box when it comes to your child's education.
- Apply a holistic thought process when deciding upon a provision.
- Think about what is right for your child now. Don't worry about whether a school will be suitable for your six-year-old child when they are 15!
- Communication is the key to unlocking a successful relationship with your child's school.
- Remember that exams are only a very small part of education. A string of qualifications is not the only way to measure a successful education.

CHAPTER 7

PLAY

Before we get started on this chapter, it is important to understand what play actually is. When most people think of play they imagine children playing with dolls houses, cars, trains or even computer games. That idea of play is very common, but it is also a very narrow view. Play is so much more than using toys and games in the way they were intended to be used.

What is play?

Susanna Millar's *The Psychology of Play* defines play as "any purposeful mental or physical activity performed either individually or group-wise in leisure time or at work for enjoyment, relaxation, and satisfaction of real-time or long term needs".[1] Here she states that play can be whatever someone wants it to be as long as they enjoy it, they can relax and it satisfies their needs at the time or in the future. It could be that someone wants to learn about an item or object, or maybe they want to socialize. Sometimes curiosity is the need that needs to be satisfied.

So, when you think of play only happening in certain ways or only happening when a manufactured toy is used, you are considering only a tiny part of what play actually is. The reason we highlight this at the start of the chapter is that autistic children (and adults) often play in very different ways to typically developing children. Our preconceptions about what counts as play or a toy are shaped and defined by our own childhoods, how other people's children are playing and those development checklists that professionals use to see if your child is following the path of the majority.

If you asked a child what a toy was, they would most likely reel off a list of expensive items they have seen advertised on television and in the

---

1   Millar, 1973

media. In fact, a toy can be anything. Pie had a large pebble once that had lots of functions, including a stencil to draw around, a person and a train! Another firm favourite was a large plastic bowl and a wooden spoon. He obviously had several mainstream toys but has hardly ever played with them in the expected way, but this doesn't mean that he didn't benefit from playing with them.

For a long time Kiddo went to bed hugging our ice cream scoop. He used a teddy occasionally, but the ice cream scoop made him feel calm, as cold ice cream is one of the most regulating sensory tools he can have.

One of the biggest challenges Charlotte has found over the years with toys isn't finding a toy that Pie likes, be it a normal household item that he enjoys playing with or a specific toy, it is the perception of other people. Comments such as "that isn't a toy" or "surely he is too old to play with that" can be very damaging to the child and parent/carer. Remember though that you know your child, and be confident that you are doing the right thing. A toy can be anything and education is everywhere. It is your job as a parent to enter your child's world and view things through their eyes and as long as it is safe, be guided by them!

Play is something that children enjoy, understand and are motivated by. For neurotypical children it's like a defined occupation that they willingly take part in. That wasn't the case for Charlotte. From her earliest memories she can remember finding play intimidating, confusing, exhausting and not something she enjoyed at all. Charlotte only played when she was pressured to. She writes the following about an experience at play group:

"I can remember attending a playgroup when I must have been about two-and-a-half. I spent the entire time sitting underneath my grandmother's chair watching what the other children were doing. When I went to nursery school I didn't have the comfort and reassurance of that chair and gradually decided I needed to mimic what the other children were doing. I didn't know why certain things had to be done but copied them and moved from activity to activity, watching what other children did and managing to convince the supervising adults that I knew what I had to do.

By the time I started primary school I found play a continued struggle. By the age of five I had poorer motor and language skills than my peers. They were aware of this and so was I. I can remember playing in a Wendy house with two other children. I was playing the role of Mum and I had been told that it was dinner time. I set to, copying the actions that I knew occurred when an adult prepared a meal. Then disaster struck,

I dropped the saucepan, tripped over the chair and landed on the play table. Everyone found this funny except me. I can still feel the heat rising up my cheeks as I realized that I was being stared at by everyone.

I avoided the Wendy house from that moment onwards but over time I struggled more and more to fit in regardless of the activity. I didn't like the feel or smell of the dressing-up clothes, not to mention the challenge of putting clothing on over other clothes. I was rubbish at art and craft, and even though I enjoyed it, I was aware that the finished product was not up to the same standard as other people's work. I dreaded it when teachers said things like 'Well done Charlotte, what is it?' Only worse than this humiliation was playing more physical games such as skipping, which often resulted in me falling over with the skipping rope wrapped around my body. I always lost at games such as 'What's the time Mr. Wolf?' because I couldn't plan quickly enough to stop moving, much to the amusement of the other children.

Play made me acutely aware of how I was different to my peers, probably more than the classroom did. As I got older my play skills improved, but in hindsight they were very much delayed and not always age appropriate. I became obsessed with dolls, and whilst I didn't engage in imaginative play with other children, I would re-enact scenarios from school, and it enabled me to process events and to learn social skills. My dolls (and cats) became my best friends; they were non-judgemental and gave me the supportive environment needed to make sense of the world. I sat my dolls in rows when they were in school and gave them all specific characteristics. I would rehearse conversations with them, and this somewhat unusual method of play was a golden ticket that enabled me to function within a neurotypical world. I would play with my dolls into my teens and continued to benefit from the life lessons they taught me, years after it was perceived to be acceptable to play."

Socializing through play
The assumption that all children want to engage in sociable play can cause many problems within families. Whilst play is something that all children need to do as part of their natural development, it isn't always something that children with autism want to do. Playing with typical toys and other children isn't always a motivator for autistic children. It certainly can be, but not always. Pie loves solitary play. To an observer the play methods he exhibits may not always seem like play. They may involve repeating the same process over and over again in a form of

stimming. For example, he might want to move a particular toy around a pre-designed route numerous times but with no aim or developed story. There is nothing wrong with allowing our children to use their time this way if they want to. This type of down time is essential for regulating emotions, processing events and making sure that any anxiety has a chance to retreat before the next challenge appears.

All children, regardless of whether they have additional needs, have individual and unique social abilities. Having multiple children adds an additional dimension when encouraging play. Organic play and interaction may not be something that ever happens, or something that takes a lot of time for an autistic child to understand.

If you are encouraging play between neurotypical and autistic children then it is important that the neurotypical child(ren) understand about autism. This is especially important for siblings. Children are incredibly flexible and caring if they are given the correct tools to understand and accept difference.

Once the neurotypical children have an understanding of autism they will hopefully be more engaged in finding ways to interact. Pie's friends B and G have always been incredibly understanding of Pie's needs because they were taught about his autism early on. When they were younger, they would sometimes have a game or activity prepared to play with Pie but understood that he might not engage at all or in an unpredictable way. Sometimes they became understandably frustrated, but generally they were able to understand that it was not something that any of them could control. These opportunities to engage with other children were incredibly valuable for Pie but also for B and G. Initially the interactions may need to be focussed more on the needs and desires of the child with autism, but over time you may be able to gradually incorporate a more even spread of activities.

How do I get my child to play with me?

This is a common question we get asked. Autistic children may not feel the need to engage in social play and may be very happy playing by themselves. Sometimes parents can find this distressing, especially when their child is younger. Parents want to form relationships with their children; they want to engage with them and share interests. The problem is they don't know how to. So here are some tips to get you started.

The first place all children learn is from their parents, and the same goes for learning to play. Whilst an autistic child may appear to want to play alone, it is important that they receive acknowledgement from their parent/carer that their game is valid. The game may appear to be non-sensical and/or repetitive but that doesn't matter; it is their play and the benefits of you joining in with them will remain with them throughout their life.

Kiddo was not interested in playing with us much at all once he hit the age of two. I would often show him toys and he would turn away, not interested in the slightest. He was quite happy playing in his own little world. So after talking with a specialist speech therapist, I started to mirror his play. If he built a train track, I built a train track. If he got cars out, I got cars out. He did start to notice I was there and would look up now and again. Once he was comfortable with me mirroring his play I would start to do some very small interruptions. I would move a train ever so slightly and say, "The train moved!" and he would move it back. The movements were always very small so that it wouldn't upset him too much, but this was his way of engaging with me. After a while he would mirror my play; perhaps I built a tower and so he built a tower. The point was, it was my job as the parent/carer to dive into his world and not expect him to dive into mine. I started taking my lead from him and before long he would show me toys and we would play with what he had chosen.

He wasn't always excited by the play I had planned for him, and why should he have been? If it didn't make sense to him why would he find it fun? Even if you spend the afternoon making reflections with metal cooking spoons and the sunlight, engaging in what they find interesting is the most important thing.

Some children will engage in an invitation to play and perhaps more so as they grow older. In order for your child to want to engage in play, it must be an attractive proposition for them. If your child does not like water for example, there is little point in trying to engage them in water play. The key for getting your child to engage with play is to start with a play activity that is something you know they will like and enjoy: something that is familiar to them, a short activity and already set up. There is nothing worse than being too ambitious. During a long hospital stay the ward that Pie was on had a brilliant play therapist. Charlotte watched her engage several children on the ward and you could see their enjoyment as they happily played, forgetting their pain and their frustrations of long inpatient admissions. One day the therapist arrived in Pie's room and decided that she was going to decorate the large window that ran the entire length of his room. She knew Pie liked *Thomas the*

Tank Engine and thought he would like to have her paint the shapes and then he could do hand prints inside. Sadly, Pie didn't like painting, he didn't like getting dirty, he didn't like change and the entire project was a nightmare. Whilst Charlotte attempted to pre-warn her that this might happen, she assured Charlotte she was the expert. That night Pie screamed inconsolably with medical staff convinced he was in pain. Thankfully Charlotte managed to convince them to allow her to wash the artwork away and normality returned.

It is important though to remember that one negative experience doesn't mean that you should never try a similar activity again. It took several attempts to get Pie to engage in any kind of creative play, but when he was 14 he started to enjoy it. This started with magic painting books and mess-free pens. Eventually Pie started using proper paint.

So, when you are trying to engage with your child in a play activity, remember:

- Set yourself up to succeed and don't make things too complex.
- Use short activities that are of interest to them.
- Allow your child to lead the activity initially so they feel safe, and gradually make small changes as and when appropriate.
- Start with one-to-one activities to reduce the need for too many social and communication anxieties.
- If at first you don't succeed, try again!

But what if you set up an engaging activity, you follow all of the advice above and it still doesn't work? If this is the case it is time to consider your immediate surroundings. The environment the child is playing in can affect their senses, moods, energy levels and focus. This is yet another reason why it is so important to understand your child's sensory profile. Check the area for noise, light and movement. Is the TV causing overload? What happens if you close the curtains? Are there too many people present? Are pets a problem? These are all things to consider and can often only be identified by trial and error. If you have a successful play session, don't forget to write down the circumstances, the game or activity and what happened in the lead up. Perhaps your child enjoys play in the company of others at a certain time of day and at other times they need to process and spend time alone. Learn as much as you can about your child.

When introducing a new toy, even if it is something that your child has shown an interest in previously, it might not be an instant hit.

That doesn't mean that they won't enjoy it at a later date. Often it can take time to get used to having a new item in their space so make sure you are not too hasty in removing toys and games that don't appear to be popular. Pie had a toy once from a TV show and it took him months to play with it and then he never stopped. Charlotte thinks it was a combination of excitement and being overwhelmed by having something he valued so much. Leave toys in toy boxes where the child can explore in their own time. Kiddo has had a train table since he was three. He went for about a year not playing with it, and then it was all he played with for months. We sometimes trial taking toys he hasn't looked at for a long time and putting them in the shed, but beware of throwing things out. One day they may want it back and only that exact toy will do.

Masking in play

Often we hear from parents who say their child plays really well. They engage with other children and play with toys in ways that mainstream society would expect. On closer inspection though, the child is actually showing signs of masking and their play is not their own original idea. Many families are refused a diagnosis or even an assessment because their child seemingly plays with others. For this reason it is important to understand what masking in play can look like.

Children with autism will often watch their peers play and copy them. If you glanced quickly you may think that they were playing in a typical way, but on closer inspection there are often several elements that make you realize that this is not an organic function. It could be the way in which they are physically playing with the toy: for example, moving a toy car along the floor but not acknowledging a play mat with a road on it. If the game suddenly changes the child may freeze, not knowing how to continue until there is someone to copy. Some autistic children will be very adept at masking, which makes it more difficult to identify play versus masking play. Look for original ideas, leading play with friends and a confidence in knowing what a particular toy is for.

Another factor to be considered, especially when considering diagnosis, is whether play stems from an original idea or is a re-enactment of something they have previously been exposed to. Many individuals with autism struggle with imagination and this can make play additionally challenging. One coping strategy adopted by many children is to re-enact their play rather than use their imagination. They may imitate a game they saw another child play or a scene from a TV show.

Autistic children can be extremely creative in play. They can design whole worlds on electronic games, they can build unbelievable structures with bricks. Kiddo builds the most incredible scenes on his tablet. I am in awe of what he builds, how he views structures in terms of individual shapes and recreates them in different media. Whilst this isn't masking play as he does this on his own, the structures are not his own original idea. They are from films, from the outside world and from pictures. This doesn't mean that he is not creative; he absolutely is. However, it is a different type of creativity. I am the same. I find it very difficult to come up with original characters, for example, but if I see another character already designed I can draw them, paint them, build them on an iPad. The original character though was not my idea. There is nothing wrong with this at all. It simply shows how neurotypical and autistic people possess different skills and abilities in creativity that can complement each other really well if we let them. There is nothing wrong with re-enacting play and no reason for this to be discouraged.

As we said at the beginning, play is a way of satisfying a child's needs. For autistic children, one of those needs can be understanding how the wider world works. This can take a lot of processing and sometimes, as for most people, physical objects are needed to help the brain work out what an event actually meant and what the overall outcome was. In the same way as you may use action figures, or even salt and pepper shakers, to plan out the tactical moves of football players on a pitch or draw a diagram of how to drive somewhere, autistic children will use props to act out social scenes to try to make sense of them.

This is a very healthy element of play and one that to an extent all children do. Play in its most basic form is an imitation of real life. Being able to process is vital for the wellbeing of an autistic person, and being able to do this with play is very acceptable. However, you might need to intervene if they are becoming anxious or if it appears they are processing an unpleasant event. They may need support as they look down on their scene in which they were involved earlier that day. They may have questions and it often helps to use the props they have chosen to explain situations, and why they happen, to them. If they ask then don't be afraid to let them take the lead whilst you act out the scene with them and help them process their emotions. If your child is processing emotions about their day, remember they do not have to be positive. Children should be allowed to express their feelings; this type of play isn't always about being positive or finding a solution. It's about the child understanding how they feel and that they will be supported by their parent/carer. Even if you don't think a child should feel upset about something they may do, and role playing with dolls and toys to make sense of their day may not always mean they are happy. They are simply trying to make sense of what happened.

Autism and interactive play

When people see their child playing alone in a room full of other children playing together, they can often feel upset or even a little panicked. Do other children not like my child? Are they being bullied? Why are they being left out? The initial assumption is that the child wants to play with others but either doesn't know how or has been socially excluded. Sometimes this is true, other times it isn't.

One of the earliest signs that a child may be autistic is a lack of interaction with others. This doesn't mean that a child with autism won't want the company of others but that they do not know how to invite themselves into a play situation or are too overloaded by large groups of their peers. It is really important that interaction isn't forced, even if it seems to be going well. Pie doesn't have much desire for social interaction. On the surface he can appear very sociable, more so than Charlotte. However, he has always exhibited a near phobic response to most children. Whilst adults are easier for him to interact with, he finds it exhausting and will quickly walk off to avoid any continued interaction. If your child is happy to play near another child that is an enormous achievement, but allow your child to interact at their pace and remember that what worked on one occasion won't necessarily work at another time. Start small and have playdates in a quiet space with one other child who is able to understand the needs of an autistic child. This will help your child to build up their confidence in social interaction. This way their efforts are far less likely to be interrupted by other peers, and your child can form positive experiences of social interaction.

This is not to say you should avoid toddler groups, as they are an important early life experience. Many parents speak of toddler groups as a stressful experience where their child's behaviour is judged. The environment leads to meltdowns and socially undesirable behaviour from the child. This stops parents from taking their child and also spending time with other parents. Whilst negative experiences can be truly disheartening, there are things you can do to help your child enjoy a toddler group.

I was extremely lucky when Kiddo was small. We joined the local toddler group when he was very young. It became obvious really quickly that he played and behaved in a different way to most of the other children. Instead of giving up I spoke with the leader about my concerns, and he made several adjustments so Kiddo and I could stay. Back then my knowledge of autism was practically zero, but when I look back I see that the simple things we put in place are adjustments that all places should make without hesitation. If you're struggling at such groups, ask for the following:

First and foremost, create an allocated safe space for your child to go and play in when the environment is too overwhelming. This will stop antisocial behaviours from your child, which are caused by fear, anxiety and the physical pain that sensory processing brings. Kiddo had a mat put down for him in the toy cupboard with a favourite toy that the parents agreed could be his nominated toy on the days we came. As time went on, Kiddo would edge further and further out of the cupboard and watch his peers. On quiet days we said his toy would be put out on a table. No other children touched it but if he wanted to play with it, he would need to come out of his safe space. He was never forced to come out and other toys were left in his space. The days his toy was taken out were very quiet and calm days where he was lovingly encouraged to spend time out of his safe space if he could. As the months went on he became more confident. He would come out to join in with art and craft. He would sit at the edge of the snack table on my lap and eventually sat on a chair one day by himself when he was ready. The day he walked over to the kitchen hatch and took the snack plates off the shelf and placed them on the table for the other children I stood in the kitchen and cried. Do not avoid these groups; request a safe space for your child.

Tell people about autism. When we went to groups I made a point of telling every adult in the room that we were awaiting an autism assessment, what that meant and what to do if they were unhappy with his behaviour. I made it clear they could come straight to me over any concern and warned them that if he felt anxious or frightened he could sometimes lash out. I was on Kiddo like white on rice. Yep, I was a helicopter parent purely to prove to other parents that I understood my child may not behave in a way they would expect. One week someone was genuinely interested in autism, so I printed off some information for them. If parents are warned in advance, they can ask their children not to shout or scream near your child and to be kind and wave if talking is too overstimulating. You need to be loud about your child's needs and you need to be proud. Being autistic is nothing to be ashamed of, but people won't learn or understand if you don't tell them what they need to know.

You don't have to stay for the whole session. When your child has had enough, leave. This could be ten minutes to start with, but it doesn't matter. These groups are essential for helping your child learn and understand about social play whilst you are there to support them. Short, positive experiences will help your child learn about themselves, learn how to self-regulate and enjoy such places in their own way. Kiddo is a master at self-regulating and was by the age of four. I am sure this is down to his early experiences in supported environments where I showed him that he could trust me and we would leave when he needed to. Leaving early is not a failure; it is a show of support for your child.

If your child struggles with parts of the sessions such as song time or story time, take them out. Engage them with another activity. Participation should never be forced. How would you like it if someone took you to a hardcore rock concert when you didn't like that type of music? You wouldn't; you would hate it and want to go home. These groups are great experience, but they are recreational and fun. Autistic children shouldn't be forced to participate in an activity just because everyone else finds it fun. Of course these groups serve a huge purpose to parents and carers as well. They provide a place to socialize and can stop parents feeling isolated. If you are enjoying spending time with other adults, leaving because of the needs of your child may not always be easy. Be prepared to leave at a moment's notice because ultimately these early experiences your child has will help them learn how to meet their own needs when they're older. Some days they will last longer, other days they won't manage it. Make sure you are aware of their needs and accept the fact that you may need to leave if it is too much for them.

By putting yourself out there, you will find parents who, although they may not have autistic children themselves, are kind hearted and want their children to grow up loving and accepting anyone who may be different to the majority. Pie's lifelong friends B and G are the children of one of Charlotte's lifelong friends:

"B and G have been a constant source of positivity in Pie's life, and they have always appeared to have an understanding of his differences, adapting their own play styles and interests when they are with him. To many they were playing with Pie, but actually they were playing alongside him. Did it matter? Nope. He was enjoying having friends and that boosted his self-esteem massively. What did B and G get out of it? They have grown up into very loving and caring friends. They have grown up with a very accepting attitude towards diversity. They have stood up for him when needed and had many amazing days where they have built incredible memories together. Who wouldn't want that for their children? Not everyone is going to be as fortunate as Pie to have friends who have shown such love and empathy but remember that meaningful friendships take many different forms."

Whilst the amount of play required may be less for an autistic child than for a neurotypical child, it is important to remember that the number of years they play for may be longer than their neurotypical peers too. This should never be discouraged, and our children should always have a place where they can play safely and enjoy the activity of their choice. A couple of weeks after his 16th birthday, Pie proudly announced he was going to play. It was truly wonderful that he is comfortable to do so because it is something that his brain needs and wants to do.

Whilst for the majority of typically developing children play is something that happens organically, for children with autism it may need additional support or prompting. If this is the case, make sure that you don't encourage them to play directly after a meltdown or shutdown. If their brains are in a heightened or anxious state, play could make things worse.

Don't ever force your child to play or be too focussed on age-guides on toys. I have known many parents who will try to get their child to engage with a toy because it is suitable for eight-year-olds and their child is eight! Allow them to play when they like and with what they like. Don't be too worried if your child tries to play in the evening before bed as in order to switch off you might find that their brain needs to be stimulated.

However hard it is don't try to control the play too much. Your child needs to feel that they are in control of their games. Make sure that the play is safe but then allow them to take the lead.

Screen time

We can't end this chapter without mentioning a type of play that causes more controversy than any other.

Screen time is a topic we hear about a *lot* in parenting. Some people see it as a treat; some people see it as dangerous. But what if someone has a genuine need for it? Many autistic children and adults get lost in their electronics. It's helpful for so many reasons yet people will often judge parents who let their children use iPads, phones and laptops frequently because they don't understand what is happening when they use it. So what does screen time actually do for an autistic and/or ADHD child?

- It helps them regulate. Watching familiar videos or listening to favourite songs over and over can actually be a form of stimming. It helps the child regulate their emotions, calm their brain and rest mentally from an arousing and stressful world.

- Many autistic children will learn in their own way, in their own space, in their own time. Educational videos can often teach autistic children more than a teacher due to their surroundings at home being more comforting, familiar and quiet than a classroom. My child learnt to read fluently by the age of four via his iPad.

- It allows the child to block out stressful external stimuli such as hospital waiting rooms, supermarkets or restaurants. They absorb themselves in their game, maybe with headphones on, and this means they can cope in an environment that would otherwise cause sensory overload.

- Autistic children can find relationships in the outside world difficult. Many form friendships online or can communicate far more easily with their friends online than in person. It can actually be their least stressful way of socializing. Of course, online safely measures must be put in place.

- It can allow children to take part in family time. ADHD children can really struggle to watch a film without becoming bored. But if they have a tablet or phone to play on, they can happily take part in family movie nights as they can occupy that part of their brain that causes boredom or understimulation. The same goes for board games and meals out.

- Just like everyone else, autistic and ADHD children need time to rest even if they are regulated. Their version of rest often means occupying their brain with games. It's simply their version of chilling out.

As with all things, screen time shouldn't be overdone. Without a doubt though, autistic and ADHD children will need these tools more often to try to exist peacefully in this neurotypical world.

Finally, we want to mention a very powerful factor that affects how our children play and also how we think they should play.

The media

The media is an area that Charlotte and Pie have struggled with over the years. They are both literal thinkers, and it can be hard to rationalize the difference between wanting an item because it interests you and because a large corporation tells you that it is the best toy on the market and you need it. Pie struggles when there is a collection of items, as if he sees ten sets within a series he then thinks that they only work if they are all together. Kiddo is the same and finds collecting things very stressful. Being able to wait is a skill some autistic and ADHD people have to work at as they find it such a struggle.

In today's society we are faced with all sorts of media, all pushing products and ideas into the heads of children who are easily influenced at the best of times. Add autism into the mix and their power can become even stronger in some cases.

If your child is into magazines and comics, there are some brilliant independent ones that don't allow product advertising so they may be worth a look. When purchasing toys that come in sets, make sure you have considered the effect having only one part will have on your child. It could be more distressing to have just one part than not have any at all. Some places such as McDonald's will let you purchase all their children's meal toys in one go rather than having to wait each week. Encourage your children to be creative with their toys; they don't have to play with them in the same way as the children on TV. Allow them to flourish and show you a world of play you never knew existed.

CHAPTER RECAP

- A toy can be anything – don't rule out the enjoyment of a household object.
- Don't force social interactions with other children as this could overwhelm your child.
- Keep play simple and as natural as possible.
- Don't focus on the age guidance of toys.
- Screen time can be very beneficial and help autistic children to regulate.

CHAPTER 8

OUT AND ABOUT

A successful day out with an autistic child doesn't often happen without some planning and consideration of a few things beforehand. Preparation is key, and whilst it might seem like just another thing to do, it will most definitely be worth it. Before you go on a day out we would suggest you think about the following.

Where to go

Choosing where you go may seem an obvious part of your preparation. You know your child best, and you know the sort of places that they will want to go and enjoy. Don't feel obliged to visit a place because other parents or professionals think that it is "the ideal place for a child with autism to go". Every child is different.

Pie has always had very specific tastes in places to visit and some of his most successful days out have astounded people. Pie loves the theatre and one of Charlotte's earliest successes was a trip to see *The Nutcracker*. Hours sitting still in a chair watching people dance. How could that possibly be a suitable place for a child with Pie's profile? He was in his own space, nobody was talking to him or giving him a demand, there were over 50 musicians playing in the orchestra (each one able to be a focus at various times throughout the performance), there was ice cream in the interval and watching the dancers and elaborate costumes gave him lots of visual stimulation. The pace of the performance gave Pie lots of opportunity to process in his own time. Whilst he went with B and G, there was no pressure for him to socialize – on the contrary he was encouraging them to be quiet!

Another thing to consider is what actually counts as a trip out. Many people may not think that a trip where you do not leave your car is a "trip out". Personally, I would disagree. Leaving the house can seem like a mountain to climb some days. A great way to offer a compromise is to leave your house but not leave the safety of your car or transport. Transport offers several sensory experiences that children often find very calming. The movement, the vibrations, the scenes out of the window and so on. Outings such as a drive-through meal or a drive-through safari can really help increase a child's confidence for experiencing the outside world whilst remaining in a place of safety and minimizing any anxiety. If you make it out of the house, you are automatically helping your child's world to grow a little bigger.

Remember, some attractions will have cheaper rates for carers or allow you to return several times with one ticket. This can be really helpful as there will be days where you buy an expensive ticket, your child has a meltdown just inside the entrance and you have to go home. It's also worth calling ahead to ask what proof you may need to bring of disability. This can allow you to enter venues through side doors or separate disabled entrances and avoid the stress of the queue. If you call ahead and explain, many attractions are excellent at providing alternative routes in without queuing.

Timing

The timing of your outing is another thing that needs to be carefully considered. Many autistic children and adults find busy places very overwhelming. The sensory experience of being in a place with a lot of other people can be extremely stressful. As we discussed in our sensory chapter, an autistic brain experiences sensory input in a different way to neurotypical people. Noises are louder, smells are more intense and lots of movement from unpredictable people can cause a visual overload and send an autistic person into meltdown. What your child can cope with will very much depend on their sensory profile; however, even a child who has mild sensory struggles may find a very busy day at the theme park just too much to deal with.

For new environments in particular, where exploring is necessary and you have no set routine of activities or sections to visit, it's often advisable to pick quiet times so that you can form useful routines with your child so they feel safer when you visit at busier times.

Travelling time also needs to be considered. There is no point visiting a soft play at 4 o'clock in the afternoon on a weekday because it is quieter, only to have to battle with the rush hour on the bus on the way home. If your child struggles with traffic jams then quieter times on usually busy routes can be really helpful. Remember, transport and transition back home can serve as very useful processing time for your child to think about where you have been and what they have experienced. For some, a disruption to this processing time can cause as many problems as a busy environment itself. Over the years I have learnt that Kiddo transitions best from a day out to home if he has half an hour in the car on the way home. He arrives home regulated, happy and ready to continue with the next part of his day. I have often driven a longer way home in order to give him that half an hour. He doesn't realize I'm doing this; he just sees it as the route to and from that particular location.

For those of you with early starters or non-sleepers like ours, cafes that open early in the morning may well become your friend. For a few years we were very lucky to have a play cafe near us that opened at 7.30 in the morning. This was a great place for us to help Kiddo build his confidence in public spaces. We were often the first in, which meant we didn't have to compete with any noise, smells, light or movement other than those of the venue itself. We would go for ice cream for breakfast because it was Kiddo's absolute favourite and it would entice him out of the house. I didn't care that he ate it so early; it was about him becoming self-motivated to leave the house and enjoy public places. Over the months we would stay later and later, and the cafe started to fill up. I supported him to stay for a little longer each week and help him desensitize to having more people around. Eventually we were able to turn up as late as 9 a.m. on a weekend and manage an hour of a busy environment without experiencing a public meltdown. Of course, it was very important to judge when he had reached his limit and make sure we left before he reached a sensory overload. Visiting places early can be a great way to help build your child's confidence and help them learn ways to deal with their own sensory needs and grow some independence.

Outings with other people

During Pie's early years Charlotte tried days out with a small selection of friends. She very quickly realized that there was just one person she could invite where both she and Pie would have a good time. J (B and G's mum) had the full knowledge and understanding that if Pie had a meltdown, or the experience was proving too much, they would need to leave early and was genuinely completely okay with that. Over the years Charlotte and J have taken their children on many amazing days out together and even those that have ended abruptly have had positive elements. Pie and

Charlotte have never been made to feel like an inconvenience, even if they have had to cancel at the last minute or stay for a short time.

We can't emphasize enough the importance of this level of trust and acceptance from people you spend your day with. Apart from the effect someone who doesn't show this level of acceptance has on you, your child will also pick up on it. Criticism for having to leave early, stimming loudly in public or complaints when changes need to be made can have devastating effects on your child and their confidence to go out and about.

Trust in those adults responsible for your welfare is essential for an autistic child when in environments they may find challenging. This means any adult who is with them when out in public. Complaining, refusal to make appropriate adaptations or criticism of behaviour are not easily forgotten and cause more anxiety about going out the next time. It can quite genuinely damage a child's self-belief. Think very carefully about whether the adults and families you choose to spend the day with are committed to helping and supporting your family.

I have many memories of other parents spending days out with Kiddo and me. I can still remember one specific situation where another mum said she wanted to learn about autism and how she could help. She didn't have an in-depth knowledge but she was committed and supported us in many a day out.

I can also remember times where other parents criticized my parenting, clearly felt I was responsible for his developmental delay at the time and didn't show any positivity towards the small goals he achieved, even when I announced it and showed Kiddo how proud I was. These were not people who were good for us to spend time with. You may be thinking, "Who would behave that way?" Sadly this is all too common, especially where parents have their own self-esteem issues and see someone they may appear comparable to. Be honest with yourself about who you should be spending days out with. They will quite genuinely have an effect on your child's development and self-confidence.

Another important element when you choose a companion for a day out is somebody who can help you practically and deal with any situations that arise. If you're attending to your child during a meltdown then you may need someone to collect bags, push chairs or even drive. Can you go with a family who would be happy to let any siblings stay with them if you had to take one of your children home because they were overwhelmed?

We have definitely been through stages where Kiddo has required a two-to-one adult to child ratio simply to ensure that his trips out do not become even more stressful during a meltdown. Your child needs you to be calm, clear and focussed. Becoming stressed yourself at their moment of need because you have no way of collecting belongings or taking them home will again cause them anxiety about going out in the future. We aren't saying that you shouldn't take your child out on your own; obviously many people have no other option. It's more about judging your location and whether you may need more than one pair of hands if the day doesn't go as planned.

With days out being a huge expense nowadays, it can be tempting to prioritize making sure you make the most of every penny you have spent trying to get there. The danger with this is that you can lose focus of how your child is coping, and it can be more tempting to try to push their coping skills just that little bit further. It can be a good idea to only go for bigger days out, where you want to spend an extended period of time, when you are confident your child can cope in the environment. Of course there may still be days where they don't quite manage it; we all have those. These bigger days may need building up to in smaller chunks. Perhaps plan in sensory breaks where you return to the car and learn the kind of regulation your child requires after certain activities such as a picnic with friends, theme park rides or soft play. Do they need time alone? Sensory activities that you can take with you include headphones for music or Blu-Tak for fidgeting. Perhaps they need free space to run in or a bounce on a trampoline. Longer days out will require more planning if you want to stay out for considerable lengths of time. If possible then talk to your child and see if a dark, quiet, safe space break would help. Get some blinds for the car windows or ask the venue for a break room. Think outside the box, build in ways for your child to regulate and, although it may take up a little time, you will really see the benefits.

Although the same level of preparation probably won't be required for smaller trips out, the same principle applies that you don't always need to stay for your entire allotted slot. Soft play is a good example of this.

Imagine you have booked a two-hour soft play session, something many of you reading this will have done, I'm sure. After a few minutes of having a brilliant time, your child is showing signs of being overstimulated. There are usually two choices here. You can either offer your child the chance to regulate their nervous system and sensory systems or you can leave very early. There is no failing in leaving at that point; it doesn't mean that the visit has been a failure. On the contrary, it is a success because you have read your child's needs and they have had an enjoyable time. They may be upset at wanting to leave early, but this is a great opportunity to talk to them about how they're feeling and what type of activity may help to regulate them. Help them learn about themselves, and help them to recognize their own signs of overload and their triggers. This is a hugely helpful skill for any child to have for the future.

Kiddo has always loved soft play. From a very early age he showed obvious signs of sensory overload that manifested in physical symptoms. His rosy red cheeks were the clearest of all. I would coax him out of the play area and take him to a quiet spot to eat an ice cream. Eating anything cold would improve his mood and reduce the redness in his cheeks, and his ability to stay and play would be extended. Of course this didn't work every time but more often than not it was a great way of helping him, even if other parents thought I was mad for feeding him ice cream at 9 o'clock in the morning.

After doing this for several months I noticed that even at a young age Kiddo would leave soft play and ask for an ice cream before his cheeks were red. I originally thought this was because he loved nothing more than ice cream. After watching him for a few weeks I realized that leaving the soft play and breaking up his play pattern was actually incredibly difficult for him. He was asking for ice cream because he had started to associate his feeling of overwhelm with a need for regulation. Several years on we can still see a difference between when he asks for an ice cream for pleasure and when it is for regulation. Nowadays he is on medication for his ADHD and his overload threshold is much higher than it used to be. He will still ask for help regulating by closing curtains, asking for cold foods or cold water or by lying in bed. Days out can be a great way to help them learn, so don't feel disheartened by leaving early. It's still a huge success to even be out and it is the start of helping your children become more conscientious.

If you're out and about with more than one child, make sure you set expectations with the other children before you leave. I used to be a childminder and would frequently take Kiddo and four other children out during the holidays. The children knew of Kiddo's needs and understood that if we needed to leave quickly there was an alternative treat or form of entertainment at home waiting for them. The parents also knew this and actually felt that it was a great way for their kids to learn about embracing the needs of others. Sometimes the days out were fine; other times we lasted an hour or two. As previously mentioned, it can be good to team up with another family who can take any siblings with them should you need to leave urgently.

Eating out

Eating out is often a fun part of a day trip and a focal point where families can come together and enjoy catching up. If a meal will be included in the day then it may be worth considering the following.

The social side of coming together to eat can be very overwhelming. All the conversations, especially cross-conversations, can cause sensory overload. If you have already been out for most of the morning your child may need time to regulate. Ask them beforehand if they would like to wear headphones to block out the conversations. If they are independent enough, perhaps they could go for a walk or sit further away from the group so that they can have time to process quietly on their own.

When you have already spent mental energy attempting to regulate in new or busy environments, eating foods that are not your usual brands cooked the way you usually have them can be a bit too much to handle. Wherever you are going for food or a snack, think about whether you need a packed lunch for your child. If the mealtime is needed for regulation and processing then familiar foods will be essential as they will not use up any extra brain power or prevent the child recharging before the afternoon activities.

Sometimes adding a meal into the day can cause additional challenges and anxieties. Pie is quite happy to eat out in a cafe, often more than eating at home. Charlotte can find it overwhelming, especially if it is an unknown place. I struggle with going to places where you can't book ahead. I need that certainty that any eating out will fit in with a pre-planned routine or my anxiety overtakes. If you know your child needs a breakdown of the day, then pre-book cafes and restaurants so they know when they will be able to eat. Most places have menus online nowadays so that your child can select one or two options (always have a safety option) before you go. Decisions can cause overload and anxiety, no matter how small those decisions may seem to other people.

During busy times always take snacks. Hunger can be a huge trigger for meltdowns and overload so always have a stash with you. Even if you're in the queue at a cafe, be mindful of your child becoming too hungry. It's not always as simple as just waiting until your food arrives; by then they could be dysregulated and it's too late.

It is always important to make sure that the venue is able to cater for your child's needs. Thankfully most places are accessible for wheelchair users by law, but not every venue is autism friendly. Speaking to the venue in advance ensures that the venue can make sure that they are able to meet any access requirements as well as allowing you to better prepare for the visit.

Other things to consider

People don't necessarily consider that invisible disabilities such as autism or ADHD require physically accessible adaptations. Things to bear in mind include:

- Are easily accessible exits available? You don't want to be halfway round an exhibit when your child overloads and needs to leave pronto, but the only way out is to keep going forward. Phone in advance and ask for permission to use fire exits, for example. You may need an ID or pass from the venue that allows you to skip sections or go backwards. If the venue is large, take a look at a map beforehand and make sure you have one whilst out and about.
- Are there sensory calming spaces? Most places won't have sensory rooms available (although this is an increasing trend) but do they have places that are quieter and darker where a child can regulate? Phone and ask as they may open closed areas for you or be able to suggest places that don't get busy that you could use.
- Does your child need to use wheelchair accessible routes? Many autistic/ADHD people struggle with hypermobility and exhaustion. Mobility buggies are large and often require wheelchair accessible venues and routes.
- Are there routes around the venue without too much visual stimulation? If your child struggles with visual overload, you may want to consider whether they will cope with visual displays. If it becomes too much on their way round, are there staff routes you could use (these are often a lot plainer)? When Kiddo was younger we were given permission to use staff corridors to escort him out in order to avoid a very distressing meltdown for him.
- Is there priority queuing? This is a big one. Waiting in a long line surrounded by other people is a sensory nightmare as well as the huge challenge of having to wait. This can be mentally draining for an autistic or ADHD person. It is not simply being impatient; it is a genuine challenge associated with being autistic for many (although not all). Call the venue ahead and find out if they will allow you to have a priority queue pass.
- Have you got a RADAR key so that you can use disabled toileting

facilities? This helps avoid hand dryers, queues and other people. All these can be hugely debilitating for autistic people and using an alternative is perfectly acceptable.

As you become more confident at successful days out with your child you will know the places and activities that work for your family. There will also be times that you visit a new place, and this will require additional elements of preparation. Involve your child as much as possible in preparing to visit a new place if that is right for them. Show them photos or websites. If it is nearby maybe drive past it so that they have an idea where they are going to.

Some autistic people need all the details they can get, others can get overwhelmed and made anxious by lots of detail. It can be hard to judge exactly what the right level of warning and detail is for a new day out. See how your child reacts to your first attempts at providing information and judge whether details will be a help or a hindrance.

Kiddo can be really keen to go to a new place, but if I give him too much information to process he can become overwhelmed and shut down. He will then refuse to go. If I'm honest, I'm exactly the same. Some days I need all the detail I can get, other days I can only cope if I have limited information. This can be difficult for loved ones as we ourselves don't always know what level of information we need. Take your child's lead and don't get frustrated. Often it's a case of the brain running away with itself and we don't realize it's going to happen. We can't help it.

It's brilliant that so many places now host relaxed events. There is less sensory stimulation and children are not expected to be quiet. We know lots of people who find these events to be life changing and it means that their child can happily participate in something that would otherwise not be possible. It is once again a matter of knowing your child and what they need.

Charlotte attended a relaxed event with Pie once and it was a disaster! Pie likes quiet and people who behave and are compliant to a set of rules he defines. This means that a relaxed performance at a cinema when people are able to get up or have regular toilet breaks would overwhelm him and result in him becoming very distressed in a way that he wouldn't at a mainstream event. Whilst we advocate any autism-friendly event, it is more important to make sure that they are right for your child.

Pie loves transport, and as Charlotte doesn't drive he has had to become used to public transport. Thankfully his love of trains has helped a great deal on this front. Charlotte always books trains in advance and where possible tries to get an advanced price on a first-class ticket. This might seem extravagant, but it means that there are fewer people, and this allows Pie to feel safe and to be able to process and regulate during the journey. Sometimes if Pie has his wheelchair then they walk rather than using inner-city public transport, which is always overcrowded.

It is important to factor in the journey when arranging a day out. The journey can give processing and regulation time, but it can also be very stressful. Make sure that your child always has enough reserves for the journey, however you are travelling.

Don't stay until your child is too tired to cope with the journey home. If you child is showing lesser signs of tiredness, don't be fooled into thinking they can cope for a bit longer without first taking the journey home into consideration.

We know that it can be hard to take disapproving looks from members of the public who don't understand the challenges your children face. When using public transport don't be afraid to use comfort items or distractions such as electronics. The journeys there and back form a huge part of a successful day and often require as much planning as the time spent at the venue itself.

It is so easy to moan when venues make a mistake that impacts on your day out. Sadly there is a lot of ignorance in the world and places don't always get it right as many of you will know. As parents of autistic children, we spend our lives battling for the adjustments they need and deserve. We can often feel worn down by it all, but it is always worth using some energy reserves to let people know when they have got it right. It not only makes the venue realize that what they are doing is worthwhile, it also helps them to realize that they are doing things right, which will potentially help other families too. Whenever you compliment a venue, you are representing a huge group of parents. Venues take pride in their achievements, and your compliment will motivate them to continue their good work and perhaps make further improvements. Never underestimate the effect a compliment has on organizations providing more services or autism-friendly adjustments.

After a wonderful day out with friends, it can seem like a great idea to head back to theirs or your house for a cuppa whilst the children continue playing. Before committing to this there are a few things that we would suggest considering.

The most important part of a day out is how it ends. Ending your day whilst your child is feeling positive will give you a far more positive platform to work from when you are planning future days out. If your child is feeling good, is regulated and has fond memories from your day out, consider whether this would be a good point to go home and continue your evening routine. Extending the day with unplanned social interaction can be a step too far. Your child may even ask or agree to extend the day, but they may not realize how tired they actually are. Sometimes it can be hard to judge when enough is enough, and there may be a part of you as a parent/carer that feels embarrassed declining an invite back to a friend's home. Ending a day on a positive note, even if that means being extra cautious to start with, will be worth it in the long run. The decision will need to be made on the day when you can see how your child has managed the day out. Before making a decision on whether to extend your day out, take into account the impact a negative end could have on your child's self-esteem and memories.

I know that I link certain emotions to films, outings and music. I don't mean the emotions that the film/venue etc. is meant to evoke, I mean the emotion I am feeling at the time when I sit down to watch it or visit somewhere new. A positive first experience will always encourage me to go back and watch/visit/listen to it again because I want to feel that same feeling. Sometimes, a feeling caused by something that isn't actually related to the film or outing can cloud my memories and all I can feel is that stressed or negative feeling. Even if the film was something that I was sure to love, if I watched it for the first time in an anxious mood I will link that film to anxiety. The same principle can be applied to visiting new places. We have taken Kiddo to places that should have been the day out of his dreams, but for whatever reason he was just a bit too anxious that day. The day wasn't very successful and that is what he remembers.

When attempting to visit a new place it isn't just about the day itself. It can be about having a calm day before, a stress-free bedtime or even just a pleasant morning at home first.

Days out will be good and bad. You might have two days out at the same location with the same plan and support in place. One could be a success and one a disaster, but remember it might not be where you have gone or what you have done. There might be an external factor that could have impacted on the day.

Linking a negative emotion to a day out is common but there are ways you can override it if you have been many times before.

In this era of technology, a scrapbook may seem a little outdated. However, Pie has about eight scrapbooks detailing days out and special events. They contain photos, writing, entrance tickets and various other mementos.

Pie struggles with poor memory and these scrapbooks are very good at reminding him of things he has done. They are also a positive record of his achievements and a great way of being able to refer back to a trip that worked and remember what worked.

On many occasions the scrapbooks have also been useful when explaining to professionals about a certain point. From a personal perspective, after a particularly tough day it is very cathartic to remind yourself of the good times. Pie will also use his scrapbooks when he is getting to know someone. He doesn't have to talk to them if he doesn't want to, but he can still share things with them.

Some children will not want to look at photos of themselves or be in photographs. This must never be forced as it will then cause them more distress to see themselves in the photo. However, photos of their favourite places and activities with friends or family members in may remind them of what they saw themselves (getting them to take the photo if they like to is always a good way of helping with positive memories) and help them link up their memory to a positive feeling.

Kiddo really varies with his desire for being in or out of photos. Sometimes he loves to take a selfie, other times it is clear he is overloaded and can't process it. If we want to remind him of somewhere we have been though, he often enjoys photos of family members or even just generic photos on a website.

Final thoughts

We have made several suggestions of things to consider in this chapter. Obviously not every day out will be immaculately planned and even if you do manage to plan every part perfectly, it's highly likely the day will find its own route. Whilst spontaneous days are often not the most positive for families with autistic members, it's more about being prepared for different eventualities and judging whether you need to go with the flow or alter the course of the day at any given moment. A perfectly planned day that is executed in a completely different way to how you had planned is not a waste of planning. Maybe your child didn't need all your strategies and backup plans that day – how amazing is that?! Some days though you will be glad you planned for every eventuality. As our children grow older they need to be given the chance to explore things for themselves and take risks. As a parent it's about being there in the background, ready to catch them if they fall hard or encouraging them back up if they stumble.

There have been many occasions when both Charlotte and I have had to cancel a planned day out at short notice. For Charlotte, this was either because of Pie's health or his autism. Never be afraid to do that. We both used to get so upset and worried if we thought we would have to cancel. We would worry about letting people down, but there was also the concern that our children would think that if they simply didn't want to do something they wouldn't have to. There was also the cost if we had paid in advance. Over the years we have learnt that cancelling is sometimes not only the best option, but the only one.

If you are going to an event with the right friends, then they will understand this, and there won't be a problem. As you learn more about your child, you learn if the reason for not attending is genuine or not. When Charlotte books an event or activity, she tells herself that the money has gone at the time of booking, but she won't book transport until the day. We have learnt that on some days there is no point in pursuing an activity as its success will be doomed from the start, and the negative implications of this will last much longer than the day itself.

CHAPTER RECAP

- Plan your day out in advance.
- Find out what works for your child, but don't restrict the sort of activities that they may enjoy.
- Check out the accessibility of a venue before you visit.
- If you are going with friends, make sure they understand the needs of your child so they are able to support you.
- Enjoy creating happy memories.

CHAPTER 9

FOOD, GLORIOUS FOOD

We always promote the message that for neurotypical parents to learn about autism accurately, they should listen to autistic adults. There is a danger with this message though that we overlook the thoughts and feelings of autistic children. Many autistic children are able to communicate very well, whether in written or spoken form. In this chapter we are including a piece of writing by a wonderful young lady describing her feelings around food. Whilst every autistic person is different, Naomi describes a number of common themes in her article that are frequently asked about by parents. Most importantly though, she explains the logic of her thoughts and why she feels the way she does about food. So for this chapter we start with Naomi's piece to give everyone an insight into an autistic child's mind and to emphasize how it is essential to trust and listen to our children when they are letting us know what their needs are.

> Sometimes bedtime is the best time. It is the one time people leave me alone. They stop asking things like *"are you hungry Naomi?"*, *"would you like a drink Naomi?"*, *"are you sure you don't want a snack?"*
>
> Why do people eat and drink so much anyway? I have things I much prefer doing like watching YouTube and playing my own games with my toys.
>
> How am I meant to eat or drink when I am doing something else?
>
> Sometimes people even want me to change rooms to eat.
>
> School do that.
>
> Why?
>
> I am comfortable and happy and then you make me move and my brain is thinking about where am I going, did I leave anything I might need, what if things have changed when I get back? What if someone touches anything?

Those things scare me.

You want me to move to somewhere, sit down and eat what you have made.

But I didn't ask for it. I did not know it was happening. No one told me I would smell different things, hear different voices and touch different stuff and now you want me to even taste things?

It is too much so I just freeze.

I can hear you but everything is fuzzy.

I am so scared. I am scared that people are looking at me. I am scared everyone is going to talk to me. I feel sick.

Why do people eat funny things? People eat things with bright colours and I can't understand that. My body is a pinky beige colour. That is a safe colour. Like a light brown sort of colour. If my skin is okay then things that colour are okay too.

You want to know why I still sometimes don't eat things that are my skin colour? Well it is just wrong. And my brain is all upset about food. When I play with my toys they look the same, they stay the same and they act the same. Sometimes I eat something and it tastes nice, it is the right colour and it feels nice and soft in my mouth. But then some days I eat what you tell me is the same and it isn't the same. It is not the way I saw it the time I liked it. It does not have the same softness and I get upset. You ruined it. Why do people do that? I order my toys in lines so when I look at them they look the same. I feel safe like that. But you don't let me do that with food. If I put it in order it makes sense. I want to know it is "right" and I need to check it. What if it is wrong and it goes inside me? That would hurt me.

That is why I have to have one thing then another. My brain tells me "this is nugget skins" and I remember what they taste like. You damage it if it has sauce or potatoes on. Then it is not nugget skins but some weird thing my brain does not know. So all nuggets are dangerous. And I get scared again.

I like soft. When I chew sometimes I get a little tiny bit to swallow and sometime a bigger bit. That means it tastes different and it does not make sense. Nibbling is safer. My teeth don't want to touch stuff because then it tastes of teeth not what it should taste like. Teeth is not a nice flavour. You know that because no one makes anything teeth flavour do they?

I feel sick sometimes. Mummy says it is hunger but I don't get it. My tummy makes me feel sick and people say it needs food when it already wants to get rid of what is in there so why add more? That does not make sense to me.

I don't think people like me sometimes. They shout at me and keep making me eat. I get scared and sad. Please leave me alone. I like it best when Mummy puts things I like near me when I am playing so my toys can look at it and tell me it is okay. I know my world is okay then.

All day long people eat eat eat. And I get scared scared and more scared. I eat at breakfast and then you want me to eat again for lunch or snack at school, then dinner, then supper.

I want it to end some days. That's why bedtime is the best for me.

Mummy asked me if I dream about food when I sleep. No way! I dream about trains. Thomas the Tank Engine is brilliant. He never eats and I like that!

Naomi Gwynne, aged 7

When I first read this blog, I was completely blown away. A young child had described so many of the fundamental challenges that autistic people face when it comes to eating. Since a theme of this book is to learn from our children, this chapter will look at many of the issues described here by Naomi as well as some of our own.

"I have things I much prefer doing."

Anyone who has ever had to coax an iPad away from a child just to show them that there is a plate of food in front of them will understand that for many people, eating just isn't a priority. I have a number of friends and family who love to eat and are considered "foodies". Personally, I see eating as a purely functional activity. I have to eat to stay alive and have energy. This doesn't mean that I don't enjoy certain foods, of course I do. I'm a chocolate fanatic and love going out for dinner. On a daily basis though I often find eating a bit of a pain. It takes up time and it takes focus away from whatever I'm doing. I just had to stop writing this book to eat some lunch and it irritated me to be honest. No one can eat the foods they like to indulge in all the time or our diets would be extremely unbalanced, but if someone told a child to stop doing their favourite activity because they have a balanced plate of healthy food for them to eat, many children are probably going to stay far more interested in their current focus. Offer them an ice cream however and I imagine they would find a way to transition from their activity to scoffing a delicious treat! The point is, if eating isn't something your child naturally thinks about or finds exciting then it might be time to make it a bit more interesting, for instance by cutting sandwiches a different way or making sure the plate has their favourite characters on it. You have to make eating more appealing than what they are currently doing. If that means letting them eat in front of the TV or whilst on a phone or tablet, so be it.

"You want me to move to somewhere, sit down and eat what you have made."

This is a lesson it took me a long time to learn with Kiddo, but once I realized where I was going wrong his relationship with food became a lot more positive. We have already talked about how difficult autistic people can find transitions and changing your focus from an activity to eating is no different. I would always ask Kiddo to come and sit at the table for lunch. Then I would ask him again. And again. After several times of asking he would eventually give in, run to the dinner table and scoff a mouthful of food, then run back to what he was doing before. Repeat 50 times until he had eaten what I considered to be enough food. To say mealtimes were a battle is an understatement. He just could not focus on eating his food. For Kiddo though it wasn't just about the transition; he also had incredibly hyperactive ADHD and struggled to stay focussed on any task. Mealtimes were a huge battle to get him to eat, and there were times when I used to just follow him round the house with a plate of food that he would take the odd piece from and eat. Needless to say, I now look back at those days and giggle to myself because the solution really was so simple. Take the food to them. Don't ask them to stop what they're doing. They are happy and content; why would you want the change that frame of mind just to make them sit at the table? Moving an autistic person anywhere occupies a lot of space in their brain. If you ask Charlotte or me to move rooms, here is a list of what will be going through our heads:

- Where am I going?
- What will the room look like?
- How will it smell?
- Will it be noisy?
- Will it be too hot or too cold?

- Will I fall over as I walk there?
- Who else will be there?

The anxiety of that transition doesn't start to reduce until you're sitting in your seat and you have acclimatized to your surroundings, by which time most people have probably finished their meal. The last thing I want to do is then add another sensory experience into the mix by taking a mouthful of food. The best thing you can do is leave them where they are and give gentle reminders to eat as they are playing. Kiddo's favourite place to eat his food is the stairs. We don't question it; that's where he is calmest and that's where he eats the best.

It is often forgotten that leaving your activity and moving to a table where there is not only food but also a lot of social activity is an absolutely massive transition that has to be made. When Kiddo was old enough to sit on a toddler chair at a table I was so excited. The idea of little lunches together filled me with joy. I had always sat wherever I had been told to and when I had been told to as a child, through crippling anxiety more than anything else. Eating at other people's homes was the absolute worst. I genuinely dreaded mealtimes in any environment that wasn't my own with people who were not family. What I hadn't realized is that Kiddo held that same anxiety over mealtimes anywhere, even at home.

The idea of someone not eating at the table with their family is too much for some people to contemplate. Perhaps this next section will highlight just how much stress this can cause an autistic person.

"I am scared that people are looking at me."

As a teenager, mealtimes had to be one of the most anxiety-provoking events of the day. I really hate it when people watch me eat. My absolute nightmare would be being at a friend's house to eat and them placing a large dish of food in the centre of the table, handing me a huge spoon and telling me to help myself. My appearance was calm at very best but on the inside I was crying and screaming and already planning my one mealtime trip to the toilet where I could catch my breath and steady my nerves. Thinking back, I think it took about three years until I felt truly comfortable eating in someone else's home. A stressed and anxious disposition is not what you want for a child when they are trying to digest food. A relaxed temperament is key. If they become upset at the idea of eating at the table or with other people, maybe it is genuinely just too much for them to tolerate. Watching someone else eat can be an incredibly overloading experience. There are sights, sounds and smells coming at you from every angle. I remember feeling extreme nausea when eating with someone whose table manners I simply couldn't tolerate. These experiences were not forgotten and led to me refusing the food that was on the table that day in the future because all I then felt when I saw, heard or thought about that food was nausea. It's commonly spoken about that teenagers don't want to sit at the table to eat, that they don't want to socialize because they would rather be on their technology in their rooms. Of course for some this is true, and maybe it is just laziness in not wanting to socialize. For autistic people it is a genuine need to be on their own when eating to keep their anxiety minimal and enjoy their food. We ask Kiddo now where he would like to sit to have his meal. He is only seven but we noticed such a huge improvement in his eating when we gave him that control. Mealtimes are first and foremost about nutrition. The neurotypical world seems to make them a social event too. Concentrate on the main aim and don't get distracted. Keep your child comfortable and happy and they will find it so much easier to eat.

"People eat things with bright colours and I can't understand that. My body is a pinky beige colour. That is a safe colour."

If you watch any cooking show on TV they talk about how different coloured foods are more appealing, they have more taste and look amazing. That's relevant to the majority of people in this world. What about the minority though?

I'm going to get all sciencey on you for a moment, but bear with me, all will become clear. In 2015 a man called Charles Spence wrote a paper for a journal called *Flavour* specifically on "the psychological impact of food colour".[1] He drew a number of conclusions that really help explain why autistic people can struggle with the colour of food. Some of his conclusions are listed below, along with an explanation from us as to why it is so important.

- "Colour is the most important intrinsic sensory cue when it comes to setting people's expectations regarding the likely taste and flavour of food and drink."

    When you are first given a food, the colour is the first thing

---

1   Spence, 2015b

you notice. It's the first sense you use closely followed by smell. If you are presented with a food that's the same colour as a food you had a bad experience with, your immediate thought is "I didn't like that last time" and the food is immediately less appealing. We all associate colours with different types of food. Red means hot and spicy; for me the colour blue means artificial and chemicals because there are not many natural blue foods. The colour of the food will trigger feelings from previous experiences. Do not underestimate that.

- "Genetic differences, such as a person's taster status, can also modulate the psychological impact of food colour on flavour perception."

We all experience senses differently. The extent of those differences depends on genetic and neurological differences in the brain. Neurotypical people and autistic people have a well-known and documented difference in sensory processing. Many autistic people are diagnosed with sensory processing disorder because their reactions are so extreme compared to the average person. One of the most sensitive senses I have is taste. I can eat a meal with my family and whilst I find the flavour level comfortable, they will find the meal completely bland and unappetizing. Memories of your sense of taste are triggered when you see food, so even if a food tastes bland to you an autistic person may find it strong and overpowering. If you put a red sweet pepper and a red chilli pepper next to each other, the colour red may remind you of eating an extremely spicy food so you refuse the sweet pepper based on colour even though it is not spicy.

- "While increasing colour variety can lead to enhanced consumption, what we see can also lead to a suppression in our appetite behaviours when associated with off colours (or colouration that is interpreted by the consumer as such)."

We often see TV chefs making huge plates of multicoloured food, which if you like lots of colour is great! If you have sensitive sight, a plate of multicoloured foods can feel very overwhelming and so your appetite is reduced because you're not enjoying the look of it. Beige food is soft on the eye, all one colour and doesn't trigger too many reactions. You're relaxed and so you eat it.

- "The latest research now shows that exactly the same food colour can elicit qualitatively different expectations concerning the likely taste/flavour of food and drink in different customers."

The most important one, folks! Just because you find colourful food attractive doesn't mean other people will. Food looks different to everyone, which means sometimes they need more support to try new foods than you realize.

"I have to have one thing then another. My brain tells me 'This is nugget skins' and I remember what they taste like. You damage it if it has sauce or potatoes on."

Mixing foods can be a very overloading experience for some who has very sensitive taste. It also hugely affects the textures of foods when you combine them. Hands up if you have ever been out to lunch with someone who can only have baked beans in a separate pot because they don't like the sauce to make the rest of the food on their plate soggy? And that's neurotypicals who do that. Combining foods changes the texture and the taste of a food. If your child develops a liking for chicken nuggets, remember that they like chicken nuggets on their own. Chicken nuggets covered in beans or potato like Naomi suggests tastes, smells, feels and looks like an entirely new food altogether. For years Kiddo ate pasta, but not pasta with sauce. When he tried it with sauce I celebrated as though it was a new food. People responded, "But doesn't he already eat pasta?" Yes, he does, but pasta *with* sauce is a whole new eating experience for him, which makes it a new food. This is why divided plates are such a success with autistic children. A plate of chicken nuggets, potatoes and beans all in separate compartments is a plate with three foods on. A plate of those foods without dividers creates the following individual foods:

- chicken nuggets
- chicken nuggets with potato on
- chicken nuggets with beans on
- potato
- potato with beans on
- beans
- chicken nuggets with potato and beans on.

You may think it is a plate of three foods, but it actually has seven if the main foods are not divided, and that is very overwhelming with a lot of different textures and tastes.

Eating two foods together can take a long time to process and feel confident in. For years I gave Kiddo a cheese sandwich with just cheese and bread. He didn't start eating them together as an actual sandwich until the age of six, which is absolutely fine. Up until that point he took the cheese out and ate that, followed by the bread but not the crust because again that has a different taste and texture to the main bread. It didn't matter. All I cared about was that he was eating.

Like Kiddo, Charlotte loves pizza. Kiddo will only eat the crust at present, which is totally finally. Charlotte as an adult will still separate her pizza to eat it. Pizza has a lot of toppings and whilst she likes those toppings, Charlotte has to be in control of the amount of sense she gets from the taste, texture and smell. Too much tomato in one mouthful can be really overwhelming, so she deconstructs the food so she can enjoy it. This is often mistaken for children playing with food. They are disciplined for not eating nicely. You must let them explore it. Table manners are not the main concern here; eating is. If by removing and separating all the pieces of the pizza it means they eat it, then why not? It doesn't stay as a whole piece of pizza whilst you digest it; in fact you wouldn't be able to tell the difference between a piece of pizza that was eaten whole and a deconstructed piece in the stomach now would you?

One of the reasons that people with autism struggle to eat unprocessed food is the lack of consistency in flavour and size. Take a bunch of grapes: each one will have a slightly different flavour and texture, which can impact on a child's desire to try such foods. Cooked fruit and vegetables can sometimes be easier to manage as the cooking process can create a more standardized texture, and the mix of the different items means that the flavour may balance out as you have the sweetest and most sour blended together. A similar problem arises in processed foods when manufacturers change recipes, and a child is unable to tolerate a food that used to be their favourite. It's important to remember that just because a food looks the same, it doesn't mean it tastes the same.

"When I chew, sometimes I get a little tiny bit to swallow and sometime a bigger bit. That means it tastes different and it does not make sense. Nibbling is safer."
Size matters, people. Well, it does in the case of food anyway. Taste is altered by an abundance of things and size is one of them. Nibbling or having set small pieces of food is another way to control the sensory input and not blast the brain with too much flavour or texture. Kiddo would only eat small cubes of cheese for years. One day he pointed to a cartoon that was making a sandwich with slices of cheese. He wanted to

try it. He didn't eat it at first but played with the feel, shape and texture. One day I showed him grated cheese, which he though was amazing! By this point he had realized that larger pieces of cheese were not going to overload him. He will still only eat potato with a crunchy outside though and in very small pieces of single small chips. If they're too long, he breaks them in two. Biting into food came much later as this was a whole new sensation and meant he couldn't investigate all the food to make sure it was safe first. For this to happen, you must foster a relationship where your chid can trust their food and trust that you have not made changes without them knowing.

As always, every child is different and for some food stuffing may be a challenge. A lot of children with autism spectrum disorder have a deficit in their proprioceptive input, and this impacts on lots of things in their daily life, including eating. It can be hard to judge how much food they should put in their mouths in one go. At one extreme there will be the children who hardly put any food in their mouth at a time and at the other those who will put it all in the mouth in one go. The reason that mouth stuffing happens is because the child cannot feel the food in their mouth unless there is a lot of food in there. Mouth stuffing also causes difficulties with oral motor skills. It is important to note that mouth stuffing is a normal part of development but should not be ignored after the toddler phase. If your child is a food stuffer there are various therapeutic interventions that can help, and a speech and language therapist or occupational therapist would be able to advise.

"I don't think people like me sometimes. They shout at me and keep making me eat. I get scared and sad, please leave me alone. I like it best when Mummy puts things I like near me when I am playing so my toys can look at it and tell me it is okay. I know my world is okay then."
This was the part of Naomi's blog that almost reduced me to tears. That a child could think that people hate them because of their sensitivities around food. Getting your child to eat when it doesn't come naturally to them is hard, no one is denying this. One thing for sure is that you won't achieve it by forcing your child to eat something they're not comfortable with. Taking your own anxiety as a parent out on your child will also only fuel feelings of self-hate and low self-esteem that will ultimately relate back to food and eating. This is not an association that you want your child to have with food. Your child needs to feel accepted, heard

and happy when it comes to food. Make the adjustments for them. Let them eat in the classroom at school, make sure their food is the same size and that no food touches another. People say they shouldn't have to do this, that it is too much effort and they don't have time. I'm telling you now: listen to your child and make the time for food preparation and you will have a lot more time on your hands when you aren't worrying and encouraging them to eat every day.

Naomi's blog is a fantastic insight into the challenges autistic people face when it comes to food. However, there are many more areas we need to touch on in this chapter.

Dieting myths

Let's start by talking about dieting myths. If I had a pound for every time I have seen adverts, social media posts or news stories where people claim that a gluten-free or dairy-free diet has "cured" their child's autism I would be a millionaire. A very cross and flabbergasted millionaire, but a millionaire all the same.

"I changed my child's diet, and he is no longer autistic!" Seriously? You think changing to gluten-free brands and soya milk is a cure for autism? Changing a diet can have hugely positive effects on an autistic person, but not because you have miraculously changed their genetics in the process. What you have likely done is one of the following:

- improved their digestive system so that they no longer feel pain after eating
- allowed your child to absorb nutrients in a far more efficient way
- freed up space in their brain to communicate and use their executive function because they are no longer experiencing sensory overload due to pain and uncomfortable digestion.

As someone who has an intolerance to gluten and irritable bowel syndrome (IBS), I can tell you that when I am having a flare up I am seriously grumpy. The pain I feel causes the most epic brain fog. It's like my brain is on fire and it makes me want to scream. I can't concentrate on anything, I can't hear people, sometimes I can't speak. The sensory experience of IBS and painful digestion is completely crippling to me. So when I switch to food that doesn't make me feel like my body is on fire then yes, I am far more delightful, communicative and calm.

The effects of the wrong diet or food intolerances on autistic people can be far more extreme than on neurotypicals. So much so that it is assumed that it is something far worse or not related to their diet at all. People become so astonished at the effects of changing their child's diet that they believe the food itself was responsible for neurological differences. It wasn't. The food caused an extreme reaction *because* of those neurological differences. Now we aren't saying that you shouldn't look into changing your child's diet. It can make all the difference. Just be aware of what is actually happening here. You can't change the neurology in someone's brain by feeding them a gluten-free, dairy-free brownie.

Changing a child's diet when they are already only eating a limited array of foods can be challenging and also dangerous. You risk your child refusing food altogether, and that's why if you have a child with an extremely limited diet we recommend that you only do this under the supervision of a medical professional. If you have staple foods that your child is happy to eat, we recommend that you do not alter these. Gluten-free food tastes different and has a different texture. You do not want to lose a food you rely on. Try with new foods and see what happens.

Having a child on a limited diet can cause concern about vitamin deficiency and countless studies have been done looking into the effect of certain vitamins on the brain's ability to function. Omega 3 has been shown to have a hugely positive effect on ADHD[2] and with Kiddo we noticed an astonishing difference, which allowed us to hold off from prescribed medication until he was a little older. Check with your medical practitioner first, but if you cannot ensure your child receives the optimal level of vitamins we highly recommend looking into it.

Aside from dieting myths, there are two other areas that we want to focus on before the end of this chapter. The first is the expectations of society around eating and the challenges this can cause for an autistic person. The second is when our internal environment (inside our body) doesn't play ball when it comes to food.

Eating and social expectations

The neurotypical world sees eating together as a wonderful social activity and we have already touched on this issue. It's well known that socializing can be extremely confusing and anxiety inducing for an autistic person. Anxiety causes shutdown, stress and meltdowns. If your child feels this way they simply won't eat and furthermore may not have the ability to

2   ADDitude Editors, 2022

eat. The brain must be kept calm and free from unnecessary pressures. Eating is done to replenish the body and allow it to function. As soon as you bring in extra demands, the brain doesn't have the capacity to process what it is eating or sometimes tolerate it. Leave eating as a quiet, standalone activity. Don't overcomplicate it.

Another social expectation is using cutlery. Eating with your hands is simply rude (apparently). What people don't realize is that having to concentrate and use motor control can not only overstimulate the brain but it can also cause a great deal of pain if you are also dealing with hypermobility. Again, this causes the brain to shut down and is simply another obstacle to your child eating. If as well as autism they have ADHD, they are likely to get bored quickly trying to use cutlery if it doesn't work. With Kiddo we didn't force him to use it if he didn't want to; we wanted a positive relationship with food and for him that meant making eating very accessible, easy and quick before he lost interest.

In fact, the need to be imaginative about not just the environment and the food being consumed but the tools being used, starts from birth, as Charlotte experienced with Pie:

"Pie had a very challenging neonatal period and feeding was always going to be a challenge. There were periods when he managed oral feeds, but these were in short bursts and dependent upon his health. He amazed the staff on the neonatal ward when he breastfed at five months of age after having been fed through tubes and IV previously. His gut needed a combination of breast milk and a specialist formula. The struggles to get him to accept any teats were hideous. He was encouraged to have a dummy during periods when he was unable to swallow, and there was a constant battle to find one he would tolerate. When Pie was four, and we were reintroducing oral feeds, the battle continued with drinking. Eventually through trial and error we discovered that he loved the sensation of drinking from a Fruit Shoot bottle. He would drink water happily from that teat, even if it wasn't the flavour advertised on the bottle. It was the lid that he was concerned with. He eventually learnt to tolerate sports bottles and straws. Nowadays if he has to then he will drink from a glass but this isn't easy because it is harder to control the amount of fluid going into his mouth at any time and can cause sensory overload."

People are expected to sit still and be quiet when eating with others. Yeah...have you ever tried to sit still and be calm when the noise is so loud and the lights are so bright that you feel such pain you could just scream? Eating out in public places presents a whole range of challenges for an autistic person. Quite often it simply presents too many. That doesn't mean it is impossible; it just means that you need to take your child's needs into account when planning a meal out. Pie provides us with the perfect example of this.

When Pie was younger, he could not go to a McDonald's for a meal. He loved the food and still does but only manages a drive thru or delivery. Any attempt to take him would result in violent meltdowns. Charlotte quickly realized that if the food wasn't the problem then it was something else. It was the environment. The next time they took Pie out for lunch, they took him to a posh hotel that was serving afternoon tea. There were no children, no loud noises or bright colours. Pie adored his afternoon tea, which they made to his taste, and the staff said they had never seen such a well-behaved child. He wasn't overstimulated and he wasn't in pain.

Nowadays if Kiddo wants to go into a McDonald's he will always say, "Music off!" Some restaurants will do it and others won't, although I'm pretty forceful on equality and I don't back down easily. Once Kiddo wanted to try even though the restaurant was playing music. He did so well but his behaviour was impulsive and erratic, and he took at least two thirds of his meal home. It wasn't the food that stopped him eating, it was everything else.

The other expectation is that if children like a food at home, they will like it in a restaurant too. Nope, not necessarily. We have already talked about how the colour of food can have a real impact on the taste and eating experience. So can smell.

How much of what we perceive to be taste and what is actually smell when we are eating has been debated for a long time. Figures such as 95 per cent have been thrown around, whereas others have claimed 75 per cent. We aren't here to debate the accuracy of these figures and studies (as much as I would like to as a psychology geek) but what is clear and very important for parents to know is that the sense of smell plays a dominant role in tasting food.[3]

Different environments such as restaurants and other people's homes can make a massive difference to how food tastes because the surrounding smells are different. I have an extremely sensitive sense of smell. It drives my husband crazy. He can't sneak a bag of crisps in the kitchen and then walk into a room I'm in because I'll know, and I'll know if he has pinched one of my favourite flavours too! When I was a child and

3   Spence, 2015a

in my teenage years, I found eating in other people's homes one of the hardest experiences; however, I did like going to friends' homes to spend time with them one on one. Socializing this way was so much easier. Whether this was masking or not I don't know but I did spend a lot of time eating food in different environments. I would eat the same meals at my friend's house as I did at home, and they could taste totally different. Spaghetti bolognese at my own house was completely different to my friend's because a) my mum used different ingredients and b) my friend's house smelt completely different. It's not to say I didn't enjoy the food because I did, but it couldn't have been more different. It was like two entirely different foods despite technically being the same meal.

There were places I found it extremely hard to eat. The childminder's was one where there were so many different children. I also found it hard in houses with a lot of pets. I love dogs and one or two dogs is fine, but combine that with hamsters, gerbils, rabbits and guinea pigs as many people seemed to have and I didn't want to eat, I didn't want to drink and in fact I didn't want to do a whole lot. It was way too overpowering. So if your child says, "I don't like their spaghetti bolognese", or "I feel too sick to eat when I'm there", if they're autistic they aren't making this stuff up. It is real.

That said, sometimes we end up in a situation where we have to attend an event where there will be food and the accompanying expectation is that it will be eaten. As we have explained, Pie adores the ritual and calmness of afternoon tea. However, Charlotte always calls ahead first to ensure that they will provide a plate of plain ham sandwiches and plain scones. People are usually happy to oblige, and this has reduced his anxiety about going out enormously. If you are going out with friends or family, maybe have a discussion about how many courses they plan to have so that you can prepare your child and maybe guide your friends if you think they are being slightly ambitious expecting that you are going to make it through a three-course meal!

Planning ahead can be helpful in other ways too. Menus are a real issue for both Charlotte and I. Charlotte will always panic that there will be an item she can't have on her plate and that in order to express this there will be the need for an additional conversation. The internet is wonderful for enabling Charlotte to look at menus in advance. She has learnt over the years to choose two different items in case one isn't available and can be prepared for the waiter to state that her choice isn't available. This method has really helped Charlotte because in the past she was so fixated on what she would be eating and processing it before it arrived that if she heard that what she had chosen was unavailable it was so overwhelming that she was unable to order anything else. This then resulted in anxiety for Charlotte as well as anyone else she was with.

Interoceptive issues and eating

Interoception is not the best-known sense. However, it plays a pivotal role in our eating and toileting, along with other internal processes. (For more information on this, see Chapter 12.) Your body does a lot of work on the inside, sending your brain signals about how you are feeling. What are the consequences though when that doesn't happen? If you don't notice or realize your tummy is growling, you won't know to eat, or you will think you aren't hungry. Equally, it is not uncommon for people with autism to find it hard to know when to stop eating. If you are concerned about your child's food intake your first stop should always be a doctor. But remember the problem may not be a clinical one; it might be a sensory one that needs management but not necessarily medication.

Interoceptive issues affecting eating (meaning too much or too little is consumed) are something that gets missed so often and it is really important to look out for this with your child. Often I will be so distracted because my ADHD is affecting me that I don't notice I'm hungry until mid-afternoon. By this point I will be stuffing my face full of snacks that are high in sugar and quite frankly awful for me because I'm beyond starving and feeling quite ill as a result. It might not just be distraction that causes this though. It could be that an autistic child or adult doesn't have an affective interoception system and that those signals of hunger just aren't happening. If you don't feel hungry, why would you eat? There are ways to get round these issues. I have alarms reminding me to eat before my hunger becomes unmanageable so that I can take my time preparing healthy food and not end up desperate for a sugar rush to stop me from passing out.

In the same vein, more and more is known about the benefits of good hydration and it can be a real battle to ensure your child drinks enough. Both Charlotte and I know personally that we get engrossed in a job and won't remember to drink until we have a headache and can't function. A lot of focus is always given to the importance of food, but don't forget drink either. Many people with autism suffer with constipation so it is essential to remember the drinks!

If you think your child has problems with understanding when they're hungry or thirsty or just doesn't feel it all, contact your primary care physician and ask for a referral to see a qualified professional (such as an OT) who specializes in this. It could make all the difference.

Finding support in the right place

Throughout this chapter we have mentioned a number of medical issues that, seeing as we are not medical professionals, we would recommend you seek advice on. However, autism being misunderstood a great deal means you have to recognize when a professional does not understand the differences being autistic can cause. When Kiddo was just over two years old I took him to see a dietician as I was concerned about allergies and how limited his diet was becoming. I explained that we were awaiting an autism assessment as I felt that would have a significant bearing on the type of advice we were given. It should have, but it didn't. I explained our concerns and was promptly sent on my way with the advice, "He needs to eat more greens." Needless to say, I declined the follow-up appointment. It can be so hard finding the right advice for an autistic child. We ended up working on Kiddo's eating plan with a learning disability nurse who recognized the issues we were facing. We made good progress and are still working on it over three years later. He eats zero greens though...

In such a neurotypical world you will find that the professional you need may not be someone who is an expert in the area you need advice for. It may not be the dietician or the mainstream speech therapist. It will be someone with an understanding of neurodiversity, autism and how brains that are wired differently often need a different approach. What Charlotte and I would say is: don't waste your time with a professional who has no understanding of these things. Go out and find someone who does.

As we bring this chapter to a close we want to remind people what the main aim is when dealing with food. It isn't about table manners, socializing over food or even being able to get out of cooking for a night and let someone else do it. It's about building your child's confidence with food and providing them with the most supportive and calming environment possible so that the idea of eating doesn't become entwined with anxiety, self-loathing and fear. This is not a road you want to go down. Just help your child to eat in whatever way they feel comfortable.

CHAPTER RECAP

- Don't force your child to eat at the table if it causes them stress. It's more important that they eat where they are comfortable and calm.
- When introducing new foods think about food textures your child will already tolerate.
- Experiment with a variety of crockery and cutlery to help your child to eat independently.
- Think outside the box. Sometimes children will like food in a certain shape or theme. If your child likes a particular character, why not be inventive with what you call the name? For many years Pie loved "Tank Engine Morning Fuel", which was porridge.
- Watch portion sizes as autistic children may well over- or undereat.

CHAPTER 10

SLEEP

Sleep. The key to your sanity, health and happiness, yet apparently rarer than unicorns. It is in this house anyway.

If your delightful cherub sleeps soundly for eight hours a night then you may want to skip this chapter. If they don't then make your eleventh cup of coffee of the day and dive in to see how many people struggle with sending their child off to the land of nod and, more importantly, keeping them there until the morning.

When Kiddo was young I heard a particular phrase quite often. It terrified me, truth be told, and each time I heard it I wondered how on earth I was going to survive until my child was 10 let alone 18 years old. The wonderful phrase is of course, "Autistic children (and adults) don't need sleep." It's an odd statement, seemingly innocent yet with the impending sense of doom that makes you ask yourself the question, "Will I ever sleep again?" Well yes, you will. It may not be whilst your child is asleep at the same time, but you will. I promise.

Before Kiddo was diagnosed (but way after we had realized he was autistic), we had our first paediatric appointment at the hospital. Naturally questions about his sleep were asked. I dutifully explained how it would take Kiddo three hours to fall asleep, that I wasn't allowed to leave the room, that eventually he slept for about four hours and how sometimes he fell back to sleep around 6 a.m. for 90 minutes. I looked up (eye contact in those appointments was not my thing at all) to see the consultant looking blankly at me, slightly open mouthed. And the next part I remember clear as day.

"Is that not normal?" I asked.

The paediatrician replied, "No."

Just, no. I wasn't sure whether to feel stupid, uneducated or just inexperienced, so I settled for feeling all three. It just seemed the safest way to be. Little did I know at the time that those were the easy days when it came to helping this child sleep; more on that later.

"I'm going to prescribe you melatonin."

Melatonin. Yes! I've heard of this! I had seen the word thrown around many parent support groups and apparently it could make people sleep. I had never heard of it before I joined these groups or started researching autism because I had no reason to know about it. But here I am, an autistic adult, though not yet professionally diagnosed. And that's why we are going to start with the common belief that autistic children and adults don't need sleep.

If there is any truth in anything said about autism and sleep, it's that many autistic people find it very hard to sleep. That's not the same as not needing it. Some need huge amounts; others need very little. Everyone is different.

Charlotte and I are polar opposites in this regard. Whether I have had a full night's sleep the night before, had a nap in the day or have been in bed all day watching TV, I will be asleep by 9.30 every night. Whether this is due to the co-morbid conditions I have is unknown, but here I am, as far as I am concerned an autistic adult, needing nine to ten hours' sleep every night if I am to feel refreshed. And I've been like it since I was a child. I must have been the only teenager I knew who drank energy drinks to give her a caffeine kick before she went clubbing, just so she wasn't exhausted by 11 o'clock. My brain gets overloaded and tired easily, often resulting in essential naps to recover from social occasions and interactions. Guys, I need my sleep. Then there is Charlotte. A managing director of a charity, a teacher, a mother to Pie and usually with several dogs to look after. Charlotte can go for several days with only one or two hours of sleep a night. She can't sleep in the day yet goes about her jobs and gets them done. If that were me (and quite often it is with Kiddo's severe lack of sleeping) I would be under the duvet for every second I could be throughout the day, grabbing sleep wherever possible. Then there's our kids. Kiddo needs sleep, but he doesn't sleep. Pie doesn't need more than a couple of hours' sleep and they can come at any time of the day or night. So, not only do you have to work out how to get your child to sleep, you also need to work out how much of it they need. So, how do you do that?

The key thing you need to work out first is whether your child is genuinely awake and raring to go or overstimulated. Whilst they are very different, both result in the same thing: a child who is not sleeping. It's really important to be able to tell the difference because your plan of action will depend on which one of these you are dealing with. Here are some signs to look out for.

Overstimulation, or feeling overstimulated, is when the brain receives too many signals from the outside world. There is too much input. It could be too much noise, light, colour or movement. It could be too much academic or social information. Ever been reading a really good book and then you just can't get to sleep afterwards because it was too exciting? Your brain is overstimulated. This doesn't just happen in the evening though, it happens throughout the day. An autistic person struggles to keep their brain evenly balanced, or regulated, all through the day and the evening. By the time bedtime comes around they may be completely exhausted, but they can't switch their brain off so they don't sleep. Neurotypicals can have the same problem but to a much lesser extent. Whereas a neurotypical person can have a bath and wash the day away, an autistic person may need several hours in a dark room with very limited stimuli from the real world. This is one of the reasons our kids adore YouTube. It's a world they can control in every way. Content, light, sound, pressing play and pause. They can fine tune YouTube to the exact correct level for their brain. A healthcare professional may recommend that your child doesn't have their iPad before bedtime, as this wouldn't be permitted in their recommended sleep routine for a neurotypical child. Yet you may find it's the only way you can get your child to calm down from a stressful day. If that's what they need and it gets you better sleep results, just do it.

Overstimulation can also come in the form of hyperactivity, and this I know about all too well. When your brain becomes overstimulated from too much input it needs to slow down, but sometimes the cogs are turning so fast they simply can't. They spin and spin and spin until eventually those cogs fall right off the gears, resulting in a meltdown until the brain levels itself out once again. This kind of activity and behaviour late at night is not a sign that your child isn't tired; it's a sign that their brain has not been regulated enough throughout the day. No one has kept those cogs in check, they haven't been kept balanced and they haven't been given enough chances to slow down. Your child needs regulating (balancing out) before they can even begin thinking about the idea of going to sleep.

But what does overstimulation look like? Sometimes it can look like your child bouncing off the walls (literally), running laps of your house or jumping on a trampoline at 11 o'clock at night. Sometimes the child can be quite still, yet emotionally very volatile. Personally, when I am overstimulated I can be really excited about anything and everything or completely the opposite sitting stone-still feeling like the air around me is full of pins prickling my skin. Either way, I am wide awake. When overstimulated people tend to react irrationally to small things, panic very easily (maybe at the idea of going to bed) and can't be communicated with effectively. Perhaps the person stops answering questions, stops listening to instructions and leaves you in a huff, feeling as though there is nothing you can do for them. No one wants to get to that point though so now it's time for some ideas on how to regulate your child, not just at night but throughout the day too, to give you your best chance of catching forty winks.

The bedroom

Let's start with the sleep environment, something I went hideously wrong with, I'm not ashamed to say. Like most parents and carers I absolutely adored decorating my child's bedroom. His first "bedroom" was a shared office with his dad so didn't really count, but his second bedroom, well that was a blank canvas. And I wished that was how it had stayed. Art and craft is my thing, Pinterest was my best friend (not literally, although it was pretty high up my list) and so off I went looking for inspiration on just how funky I could make Kiddo's bedroom look. I painted roads, a sky and grass. I stuck stickers of cars on the walls, helicopters the lot. I had so many compliments, I felt like the mum who had conquered it all. And then Kiddo never slept again.

What we didn't realize was that in order for Kiddo to keep his brain calm and regulated, he needed as little stimulation in his bedroom as possible. He got enough of that throughout the day in the outside world; he needed a safe, calm space where he was in control of how much information entered his brain. So, eventually when we had worked this out, we moved him to a new room. We painted the walls a plain colour and had no drawers or wardrobes in there. We had a cupboard that was built into the wall turned into storage and he had a bed. Nothing on the walls at all. At first we felt awful as though we were somehow being neglectful by giving him a plain bedroom with nothing in it. Then we saw how often he took himself away upstairs into his room. He would go up with an iPad and play games or maybe just stim for a while. It was then I felt his relief; I felt his need to be away just for a little while so that those cogs slowed down in his brain. The only difference was that when I was a child I liked having photos, decorations and pictures on my walls. I didn't however sit for hours on YouTube. I had created my own world in my room as a kid and now he was able to enjoy his. Time went on, and we even removed the bed because he jumped through it. He now has two mattresses on the floor in his room. Sometimes I go and sit in the dark with him, and he loves it. I love it. It was never about making myself feel like a super parent, never about what a neurotypical child might have wanted. It was about truly asking myself what my child needed and trying out different ideas. If something isn't working then try the opposite.

Obviously though, as we echo throughout this book, everyone is different. When it comes to sleep, Pie is completely different to Kiddo. Pie cannot sleep at all unless he has the following:

- two fans on
- Classic FM playing in the background
- an audiobook on
- the bedroom light on
- a spotlight on
- a plastic sheet on the bed
- a duvet cover to sleep inside.

The two could not be more different. It's about finding out what environment suits your child the most. As long as they can safely be left to sleep, don't be afraid to think outside the box. After all, society can judge you when you're exhausted or when you've had sleep. Personally, my responses are a lot sharper after I have had my beauty sleep.

Daytime sensory breaks

As previously mentioned, it's not just about the sleeping environment itself. Being regulated at night comes from being regulated during the day, and frequently at that. For this, sensory breaks are an absolute must. These could involve some quiet time sitting on your own in a safe environment (perhaps after a particularly busy activity) or a set of activities designed to balance your senses back into equilibrium. Whilst we won't go into detail in this chapter as to what a sensory break involves, know this and know it well: your child does not need to be showing any outward symptoms of being over- or understimulated in order to need a sensory break. For you all to truly feel the impact at bedtime, they must be offered throughout the day, including in school time, and the child must feel confident that these opportunities will be given to them. For more information, see Chapter 5 on sensory processing.

A bedtime routine?

So, once you have the sleep environment sorted, the next thing is to think about how you approach the idea of bedtime. How do you start to talk about it with your child and how do you get their mind and body ready to switch off after a long day? In other words, what bedtime routine are you going to use?

Anyone who has approached professional services will know that this is one of the first things they will thrust into your hands: timetable planners, pictures of children brushing their teeth (pah!) and the tools to create solid rituals for how we wind down for bedtime. For some people this is hugely successful. If your child likes to see pictures of what they should be doing and pictures of what the next step is then we whole-heartedly encourage you to use them. Stick a picture routine on your bathroom wall, hand your child the pictures one at a time, whatever works for you. *But* (and this is a big but), here is the important thing you should be acutely aware of that many professionals are not.

Fixed routines can often make things worse.

When our family was referred to our first of many professionals who would advise us on sleep, we were asked to keep a diary (I can hear you all groaning from here) and to make sure we had a fixed routine where Kiddo would know exactly what was happening and at what time. And it was a total nightmare. The minute he saw a picture card or saw me getting ready for his bedtime routine, he would end up in a horrific meltdown. He wasn't calm; he was full of anxiety. He had had too much warning of what was coming, and he was scared. Sometimes having a long time to process something can be a bad thing. Very quickly we stopped with the picture cards and routine, but we were strongly encouraged to continue with them by professional services who said that more time was needed. As Kiddo's parents we knew this wasn't right. We very quickly came to the conclusion that we needed a professional who would listen to us. So we asked to switch to someone else and lo and behold we were given someone who completely understood that for Kiddo, picture-based routines and timetables were a no go. Of course by now I had plastered Velcro all over the walls of my house. Brilliant. The point is, if something doesn't work, do not try to force your child to adapt to it. Sure, give it a reasonable go, but if it is causing your child distress, to self-harm or to be upset then STOP. You cannot push past these things without causing your child significant damage. People say to me, "Oh but they settled eventually." How much damage was done to that child in the meantime? Are they truly settled now? Or are they just masking their behaviour from fear to appear as though they are accepting of the routine? These are the important questions we must ask ourselves as parents.

So, if routines aren't for your child and too much warning causes heightened anxiety, what should you do? The answer is the complete opposite of everything you have ever been taught. One evening we decided that Kiddo wouldn't have a bath, wouldn't have a story unless he asked for one, wouldn't go to bed at the usual time and wouldn't be given any warning about how long it was until bedtime. We gave him a glass of milk, handed him a toothbrush in the living room to clean his teeth and then just sat downstairs for a bit. I went upstairs and got his pyjamas out and then said "upstairs" (not, "time for bed" or "bedtime"). Up he went, put his pyjamas on and lay down. I asked him if he wanted a story, to which he responded by throwing the book across the room. We sat down together in the dark, and half an hour later he was asleep.

Now this being the first night we tried it, and it going so well compared to the routine-based nights, we weren't left thinking we had conquered the world. The fact that the next evening when we gave him his milk he screamed his head off and had a meltdown shows how he was struggling with any warning signs of what was to come. So we started giving him choices. "Milk or story?" "Bath or no bath?" Eventually after weeks of this (and it really does take time) Kiddo told us what he wanted his routine to be, and it changes frequently. He goes through phases of wanting a bath before bed or wanting it at another time of day (or not at all, let's not sugar-coat this). He changes the type of pyjamas he wants; maybe he wants to sleep in his clothes. Now many years on, I will hand him his milk and he says, "First milk, then brush teeth, then bath and bed." It all came from him. He designed that; he had control and choice. Most importantly he knows he can change it whenever he wants to.

Regular routines are very successful for many people; some autistic people thrive on them. Make no mistake though, many do not. Autistic people are not broken and do not need fixing; they should not be forced into something they find distressing, no matter what a particular professional might say. So, work out whether strict routine is right for your child, or following their lead is much better. Ask yourself whether anything they are requesting is really worth an argument over (do they really *have* to sleep in pyjamas?) or whether you would just prefer them to sleep. Whatever you may have learnt about bedtime as a child, you may need to wipe it and start again.

Before we move on from routines there is one final point we need to make. Sometimes activities that we expect to be calming for our children are in fact the complete opposite. Take having a bath, for example. For me it is usually relaxing but depending on the day I have had it can sometimes be sensory hell. Showers in particular are something I struggle with because parts of my body are warm, and parts are cold. Bear in mind that what may be calming some evenings for your child could be invigorating or even painful on others. Sensory experiences can change; they don't always stay the same. On the evenings where maybe the usual activities don't work, make a note of what and any reason why (e.g. activities from earlier on in the day). We have talked about this already in Chapter 5: sensory profiles can change on a daily basis and this is something you need to be aware of.

Sleep medication

So, you've tried all of the above, you've barely slept for three years and now you are completely at your wits' end. Sleep is a distant memory, your eyes sting from tears of exhaustion and you look like you have aged about 40 years. Wow, do Charlotte and I feel you here. There is a reason sleep deprivation is used as a form of torture; it is simply beyond hideous and that's why, sometimes, medication might be needed.

The environment is one thing, but medication has its place. Melatonin is often widely misunderstood, and I find this is because consultants don't take the time to explain it. After a *very* long fight to be referred to a sleep specialist in a large London hospital, I also learnt that sleep and sleep medication are hugely misunderstood by a large number of healthcare professionals. Not only this, but some professionals genuinely don't seem to understand what a consistent lack of sleep does to you mentally or physically and therefore don't give it the attention it needs. Once you have experienced a chronic lack of sleep you will never forget it. You will never overlook someone's exhaustion again and you will never respond with, "Yeah we're just all knackered, aren't we?" No. No no. True sleep deprivation is hellish. I've come to realize that parents of a newborn baby get the care, attention and love that many of us still need ten years later. We don't get it though, because our situations are so often completely misunderstood.

Before we dive into "the science", please remember that neither Charlotte or I are doctors or medical professionals. We are looking to provide simple explanations of things that often are not presented to parents. We are referencing medical and autism websites to help explain these definitions.

So what is melatonin, and how can it help you in the fight against the wide-awake club?

According to the NHS, "Melatonin is a natural hormone that is produced by the pineal gland (located in your brain). It helps control your sleep cycle. The body produces melatonin just after it gets dark, peaking in the early hours of the morning and reducing during daylight hours. Melatonin acts on receptors in your body to encourage sleep."[1]

Sounds great, doesn't it? Until of course your little cherub doesn't produce enough of the damn thing. Then the problems begin. We have already spoken about the many environmental reasons autistic children and adults may struggle with sleep, but when you have tried all of those it is time to consider whether irregular melatonin levels might be the cause of the problem. The National Autistic Society states that, "irregular secretion of the sleep hormone melatonin, which regulates sleep patterns, or having atypical circadian rhythms (body clock)"[2] could well be a cause of sleep problems in autistic people. Keep a sleep diary and get in touch with your healthcare professional. Most consultants won't issue the drug without evidence that you are trying all the environmental changes first. Even if these changes don't appear to have a direct impact on sleep, they will help your child in other areas so it is definitely worth doing anyway.

Alongside melatonin there is also Circadin, another common drug you may find prescribed to you. The main component of Circadin is melatonin, only this drug releases the hormone gradually throughout the night. Melatonin will give you a hit of the hormone and help you fall asleep, but it won't necessarily keep you asleep. The aim of Circadin is that when taken as a whole tablet, it slowly releases throughout the night. There's a teeny tiny problem here though. For most autistic children, the tablet has to be crushed and taken with liquid as swallowing tablets is not something that is easily understood or accomplished. Crush it and it releases a whole lot quicker, meaning your child is likely to wake after a few hours.

Back to the drawing board...

When Kiddo eventuality went from falling asleep in three hours or more to falling asleep within 20 minutes of his head hitting the pillow (or mattress, this kid hardly ever uses a pillow), I felt like I had won the lottery. Screw the millions that people were winning every week; I had

1   NHS, 2019
2   National Autistic Society, 2020

sleep! Beautiful, glorious, delicious sleep! And then I woke up. Literally. Kiddo was only asleep for approximately three hours.

I cried, a lot. I had come so close. So close to removing the never-ending headache, so close to actually building my immune system, so close to feeling the one thing I would never feel again. Awake. I realized that day how many hurdles we needed to jump in order to manage a minimum of four to five hours every night. I was back to writing the sleep diary.

The next few years were trial and error. If you suddenly recoiled into your seat at the word "years" then don't panic. Kiddo has major league sleep issues and Pie is the league champion of that league for sure. We worked hard with our medical team to find the best solution and tried a few things. It was really hard and at times I begged for the simple fall asleep and grab three hours routine. But it wasn't sustainable for the rest of our lives. Some medications played havoc with Kiddo, and it was then that we learnt a great deal about him and what makes him tick. I won't be mentioning the drugs we tried because it's the lessons behind the process that I want to explain to you all.

Having maxed out the melatonin, we tried a drug that had a sedative effect. Success! Until his body built up a resilience to it and we were back to square one. So, we tried another sedative. Disaster doesn't come close to describing our lives over the following few weeks. It became clear that the previous sedative was a one-off drug that helped sleep provided he didn't have it all the time. A different sedative made Kiddo more hyperactive than I have ever seen. I'm not exaggerating when I say I don't know how we kept him out of hospital for those few weeks. He didn't sleep, his behaviour was dangerously hyperactive, he was aggressive and almost delirious at times. This was on a dose that was half the lowest dose you could start on. But what was it that caused the effect? Kiddo has a diagnosis of ADHD (both hyperactive and inattentive). His brain lacks a stimulant effect, and this stops his brain from acting quickly before he "jumps". All we did was remove the tiny bit of stimulant he had in his brain by crushing it with a sedative. It was then that we learnt that Kiddo would require stimulant medication to help him handle his ADHD in the future. As for the original sedative, who knows why that worked; I didn't try to find out.

The point is, just because melatonin or another sleep medication works for someone else's child, it doesn't mean it will work for yours. Everyone's autistic brain is wired so differently, every brain reacts at different levels. Kiddo reacts to medication very quickly, same as me. Many autistic people don't react to medication at all and require much higher doses just to get even the slightest effect. Circadin made no difference to Kiddo at all; when Pie tried it he became aggressive. This is why it is so important to get medical oversight when trying any sleep medication.

You've changed the sleep environment, helped your child regulate throughout the day and you've (hopefully) sussed the sleep medication. Surely nothing else can affect your child's sleep, right? Grab another coffee, we have a lot more to talk about...

Transitioning from a cot to a bed

One of the questions I get asked the most on my blog is, "How do I transfer my child from a cot to a bed?" A fair question as well: Kiddo didn't even understand what sleep was by the time he was climbing out of his cot. He wasn't yet two years old the first time my husband opened the door after naptime and found him diving into his clothes drawers in his bedroom. So, what practical steps did we take to move a child from a cot to a bed when they had no understanding of bedtime or the need for sleep?

- Make the bedroom area absolutely and completely safe for a child with no danger awareness. Attach everything to the wall, remove nappy creams and baby wipes, use window locks, the lot. Your child will be left alone in that room (even if they still share with you) and will be mobile around that room possibly even when you are asleep. There can be *nothing* in that room that could cause them harm. We even removed most of his toys. Remember, a plain room with a bed in it is no bad thing.
- Consider getting a camera monitor. You will not want to be checking on your child every time you hear a noise. If they work out that crying or loud noises make you come running, you're stuffed. Nevertheless, you need to be able to see what they're up to because, and I don't know about you, mysterious noises still make me run through to Kiddo like Usain Bolt. As an extra tip, make sure they can't reach the monitor and the wire is nailed into the wall. One time Kiddo got hold of it and the monitor alarm woke me up. Being half asleep I glanced at the screen to see two eyes staring into mine like some kind of scene from *The Shining*. Needless to say, the whole house was awake by the time I had finished screaming. Moving on...
- Place a stairgate on the bedroom door and at the top of the stairs. The only way a child with no understanding of sleep will come

to learn that bedtime means actually being in a bed is if they're not allowed out of the room. There is a great deal of controversy around the use of stairgates as children get older, but at such a young age when stairgates would still be used for neurotypical children it's acceptable. Now what I don't mean is that you lock the gate and just leave them in there. That's distressing. You need to develop a way of encouraging your child into bed, then encouraging them back into it when they get out, then slowly removing yourself from the environment. For Kiddo I would first get into bed with him. After an amount of time I would get out and sit next to the bed. Whenever he got out I would tap the bed and encourage him to get back in. I didn't use many words; I wanted him to know that now was quiet time. I kept doing this until he had managed a few minutes in a row in bed without me. Then I moved towards the door and did the same. The big one was when I moved outside of his room and sat on the other side of the stairgate. The physical barrier was a real worry to him, but he had to learn he could be safe without me. I developed a little phrase that I calmly and quietly repeated until he calmed. I just said, "Mummy here. Kiddo safe." Eventually I moved to the point where he could see my foot on the other side of the gate from where his head lay on the bed. This meant I could watch things on my iPad and message friends (remember at this point bedtime was taking three hours plus). Eventually he learnt that when the gate was shut, it was time for bed. Once he realized that, and we had his melatonin working for him, he was usually asleep before I got to the point of leaving the room and now, five years later, I sit next to his bed and he falls asleep without too much fuss. Usually.

- This is really important. Once they are asleep and you head to bed, make sure the stairgate is opened and your bedroom door is open. You do not want to stop them from being able to get to you in the night. This will make bedtime worse and could cause huge safety issues. If they come to you in the night, repeat the previous stages until you feel that it is a reasonable time to get up. Set that deadline for yourself. When Kiddo was younger he was not allowed downstairs before 4 a.m. As he became older he made far more noise upstairs and his dad needed to sleep for work. He was also far more likely to return to bed after a burst of energy downstairs. You'll have to follow your own nose with that one.

This may not work for everyone, but the principles of safety and understanding what time of day is for bed are things you need to get right and may need to work on for a while. You know your child and what works for them.

"Have you tried using a Gro Clock?" That question is listed in my book of all-time-hated questions about parenting an autistic child. For those of you who don't know what a Gro Clock is, let me describe it for you. The clock has an electronic face that displays the time and either shines yellow with a picture of the sun, or blue with a picture of the moon. They can be absolutely fantastic at teaching children when it is day and when it is night. You can programme the sun to set at whatever bedtime you choose and the sun to rise at whatever wake-up time you choose. Many parents have had huge success at explaining to their children that when the sun is on the clock, they're allowed into Mummy and Daddy's room. So, in my desperate hour of need I tried one with Kiddo.

Words cannot describe the meltdown that happened as we watched the sun set on that clock. Kiddo was all smiles looking at the sun, and then slowly it moved away and then disappeared altogether. You see, when an autistic person watches something like that sun leaving, they assume it is gone for good. Luckily, I got to the clock before Kiddo so I was able to sell it on to another family who it worked wonders for. But ask many a family with autistic children and you'll likely hear tales of woe. Either that or that it made absolutely no difference whatsoever.

So, whilst many parents smile smugly during season changes and put pictures of their Gro Clocks on Instagram for you to swear at, I suggest you invest in a seriously good blackout blind and carry on with your routine as usual. Hour changes can really mess our sensitive little ones up. Remember that melatonin is produced when it is dark so your child will need time in a dark, quiet space before heading to bed in the lighter months. You'll need to see if you can jump start their brain a lot more than you do in the darker winter months and give them time to adjust to the transition between day and night.

Sleep routines and co-morbid conditions

Of course, there is always the added complication of co-morbid conditions that impact on a sleep routine. Conditions such as ADHD and epilepsy are common in autistic people and with them come core symptoms that can interfere with sleep as well as medication that can do the same. Over the years Pie has become more complex and some of these additional conditions have had an impact on his sleep, in particular his epilepsy. When he has a grand mal seizure this can make him very sleepy for hours afterwards, but if this happens in the afternoon it often means that he will be awake come bedtime. Anti-epileptic drugs and Pie's anti-psychotic medication can cause drowsiness, but this doesn't always result in sleep and is more likely to make Pie irritable. The brain's threshold to not have a fit is lessened without sleep and for Pie this is a challenge as he needs such small amounts of sleep. Charlotte has tried several sleep medications over the years without much success. Melatonin made him more alert and less able to sleep. As he reaches adulthood it is now a matter of following his lead with sleep whilst being mindful of juggling his various disabilities and medical conditions.

The final thing to take note of on the topic of sleep is recognizing the point at which your child is old enough to take the lead. We mentioned at the start of the chapter all the things that Pie needs in order to manage any sleep at all. There is no way Charlotte would have found out that it worked unless she had trusted Pie to show her the way. To you it might seem bizarre, but to our children it is what they need. At the end of the day, it has to be about what works for your child. As long as they are safe and getting the sleep they need, ask yourself: does what they're asking for really matter? So what if they sleep in their clothes? So what if they sleep under their bed (incidentally this is usually for sensory reasons)?

Broaden your minds on this one; the aim is for our kids to sleep safely. And maybe reduce our intake of caffeine just a tad...

CHAPTER RECAP

- Look at the sleep environment and follow the child's lead on what they find relaxing.
- Regulation for sleep is a process that goes on throughout the day.
- A fixed routine is often not the answer.
- Allow for the side effects of any drugs for other conditions that your child may take.
- Don't dismiss the idea of medication, but equally don't feel that you have to try it.

CHAPTER 11

EVENTS AND CELEBRATIONS

Whether we like it or not, life will always have gatherings, events and celebrations. Whilst some people adore such events, others find them very challenging from both a social and sensory point of view. For an autistic person, attending a big social event or major religious festival can be overwhelming and exhausting, but not impossible. In this chapter we talk about the differences in how autistic people view and experience events such as birthdays and weddings, and list some general principles to consider when planning to attend an event with an autistic person.

Celebrating birthdays

Let's start with birthdays.

When you think of a child's birthday party what comes to mind? Balloons? Cake? Party games? Trips out? Birthday celebrations are not only considered a hugely positive event, over the years they have been commercialized and turned into large money-making machines.

The world is filled with external pressures on what a birthday party should look like. After all, who wouldn't love fun and games, party food and lots of friends all there to celebrate you turning a year older? As it turns out, quite a few people don't like it, and that includes children.

When Kiddo turned one I threw him a huge birthday party at home. I was so excited! We had a *The Very Hungry Caterpillar* theme and I went all out. All out with the food, the decorations, the cake, the lot. As a one-year-old Kiddo was more concerned about playing with his own toes. That party wasn't for him; it was for me, and I completely accept that.

Fast-forward a couple of years and I remember throwing him a birthday party that changed my view on his birthday for good. For his fourth birthday we hired out a soft play cafe and invited around

30 children. I genuinely believed back then that he deserved the works. That year had been tough for us. He had been diagnosed with autism and ADHD, but that wasn't the hard part. The hard part was changing my parenting style to adapt to his needs. This party was a turning point for me. I adored my child, and I was giving him everything he deserved for his birthday. There was only one problem. I hadn't actually considered if the birthday party I had planned was a birthday party he would want.

I remember watching him hide by the toilets as his friends arrived. He liked these children yet wouldn't go anywhere near them. The noise and the movement in particular were just way too much for him. He spent the whole party sitting in a side room. Whilst I sat with him and felt like I had been punched in the gut, something happened that opened my eyes to what he truly wanted. A couple of children appeared at the door of the room with a lovely mum. She said they had been wondering where Kiddo was, and they had brought presents. Kiddo's eyes lit up and so I said he could open them now. For the next 45 minutes five children sat and played with the Play-Doh present he had been given. It was the most beautiful sight. Through the door was an exciting party with slides and climbing. Yet here was the birthday boy sitting with a few other children, all quietly playing.

I realized so many things that day, but the most important one was that I needed to put myself in Kiddo's shoes when it came to planning his birthday. What did *he* want? I imagine you're thinking that I never threw him a birthday party again. Well, you'd be wrong. I did, but wow was it different.

A few months before his sixth birthday, I said, "Kiddo's birthday soon! Would you like a party?" His verbal skills were not developed enough yet for him to answer me and I knew this. What I was looking for were signs about what a birthday party meant to him. Sure enough, over the next few days he began watching YouTube videos of birthday parties. He would smile and laugh, so I made sure I could see exactly what was on screen at that moment. He smiled at balloons and cake. Okay, I can do that, I thought. Then a particular video kept being watched of children on a bouncy castle. Yes! Totally doable! At that moment, as I was planning a large hall with a bouncy castle, I was taken back to his birthday two years before. He didn't come out of the side room.

But he seemed so happy when I listed balloons, cake and bouncy castle for his birthday. "Friends?" I asked. More smiles. How was I going to do this? Turns out very easily: I just booked a venue with multiple rooms. I made him a safe space with colouring and balloons in. He could come and go as he pleased. We had another room for food, and I made lunchboxes so he could take his into his safe space. We didn't sing happy birthday as this had caused a meltdown in the past and when we got home he blew out candles on his cupcake. It was perfect.

What I hadn't considered was that Kiddo had grown up in the two years leading to this party. It didn't need to be an all-or-nothing event, it just needed to be an event that was tailored to him. Perhaps that would be a day out with family, perhaps it would be a huge party with a safe space. Whatever it is, birthdays need to be adapted from the so-called norm so that autistic children can enjoy them. Even more importantly, parents need to accept these adaptations and sometimes limitations. A successful birthday is one that is thrown for the child in question and not just one the parent has always dreamed of organizing.

A couple more years on and now he really looks forward to his birthday. We have a few friends over for cake, balloons, presents and his current favourite activity, a piñata. Who knows if we will throw him a big party in the future? Really that's up to him.

As a child Charlotte found attending someone's birthday party overwhelming, anxiety inducing and a sensory processing nightmare. There was only one thing worse than going to a birthday party and that was attending her own. This was down to the additional pressure of being the centre of attention and the person who was expected to be enjoying themselves. As an adult, birthdays and birthday parties continue to be anxiety inducing and something to be endured rather than enjoyed.

There is one birthday she can enjoy though, and that is Pie's. When he was born she never imagined that she would get to celebrate one birthday and as we write this he is heading towards his seventeenth. Pie enjoys his birthday much more than Charlotte does. He has always had a celebration that is tailored to his current interests and needs. Over the years this has ranged from hardly acknowledging his birthday, to attending a West End musical, to a takeaway at home.

Charlotte knows that there are certain things that Pie needs to do on his birthday. He needs to see his friends, he needs to know in advance what he is doing (no surprises) and most of all he needs time to process, which is spaced out throughout the day.

Charlotte has learnt over the years what works and, as I have, she has made mistakes. What is important is that you learn from them. Remember that your child's birthday, whether they love or loathe it, is their day and they will have their unique but perfect way of wanting to celebrate it.

Weddings and other big celebrations

Birthdays aren't the only celebration people choose to hold on such a large scale though. Weddings are often huge luxury affairs with more sensory input than an autistic brain can handle. There are so many unknown factors with weddings for a person with autism and their parents/carers. By definition the wedding is about the couple getting married and this means that it could be rather awkward to phone the happy couple and list your requirements. Before having Pie, Charlotte politely declined several wedding invitations or just attended the marriage ceremony. She knew how much she would struggle and felt it would not be right for this to impact on somebody's special day.

There is music, noise, movement and cameras flashing, and traditional outfits are often among the most uncomfortable clothing you could imagine. At my own wedding, I wore a dress that was light and airy and didn't make me feel like I was being pricked with a thousand pins. I loved it. When I was trying it on, the manager of the shop couldn't believe that I had chosen the dress I did. I had tried another that was absolutely stunning. I lasted four minutes before I felt suffocated and trapped – I also couldn't sit down in the bloody thing! She told me how beautiful it looked, and she was right: it looked amazing! However, it would have ruined my entire day. Obviously when you are someone's bridesmaid you wear what they tell you. I'm lucky in that, apart from shoes, I have never been asked to wear anything hugely uncomfortable. For autistic children though, any role in a wedding must be considered carefully.

Both Pie and Kiddo have been page boys in the past. For both it took an immense amount of planning. Kiddo was very young, not quite two years old, but his needs were clear and he was on the pathway for an autism assessment. Our first challenge was getting him to feel comfortable in his outfit. Luckily my sister-in-law and her fiancé were very understanding and gave us an idea of the outfit they would like him in. Off I went to find shirts and jackets that he would tolerate.

On the day itself we kept him away from the hustle and bustle of everyone getting dressed up and excited. In those days his grandparents were able to cope with him because he was still so small. We met him at the church door where he was looking a bit bemused but was happy to see me as I stood at the front of the queue of bridesmaids. The music started playing for the procession. I'm guessing this is what threw him, as he suddenly threw my dress upwards and flashed my underwear for the priest and half the congregation to see. After a moment of comforting he decided to come out from under my dress and we started to walk. That is, until Kiddo started to run. Seeing his daddy standing at the front of the church, he escaped my clutches and proceeded to sprint down the aisle at speed towards his dad (fortunately, he was still small enough for this to be adorable). Just as he started to divert towards the altar, his dad caught him, carried him to the back of the church and gave him to his other grandparents who promptly took him home. We didn't attempt to make him stay for the service and my parents strongly advised we didn't try to take him to the reception. Just that ten-minute segment was enough for him and his auntie and uncle were delighted that he had even managed that. All the planning was worth it just for him to be able to make an appearance, be himself and go home afterwards. Sometimes though our children surprise us and manage things way beyond our expectations.

One of Charlotte's closest friends got married when Pie was seven. She was delighted for her when she got engaged, and within a matter of weeks the bride and her then fiancé asked Pie to be a page boy. This was a moment of pride and also trepidation for Charlotte at how Pie may struggle to fulfil this role or what would happen if he did something that would be detrimental to their day.

She needn't have worried; everything was well planned and Pie was given the opportunity several times in the day to have a break. The wedding breakfast was early in the afternoon and as soon as it was finished, they left. There were no hard feelings that the family left so early and no obligation to push Pie more than he could manage. The entire experience was one of Charlotte's happiest memories of Pie's childhood. This was thanks to the understanding of the couple and the allowances and adjustments that were made to ensure that Pie could carry out his role. It would not have worked had he done it for another couple or, potentially, at another time in his life, but on that bright, sunny July day, it was simply perfect.

Planning is essential when attending big events. You don't have to send over a list of demands, but by all means, if you are given the opportunity to do so, be open with the couple and see how things might work. Alternatively, do not feel bad if you have to decline these events. Be honest and explain. As with so many things in this book, communication is key.

Funerals

As sure as the sun sets at the end of each day, so life comes to an end and with this comes the event of the funeral. Funerals are really difficult for everyone but how we handle that difficulty can be completely different.

For some autistic individuals, the finality of death makes grieving a much easier process than for a neurotypical person. Often an autistic person will find the lead-up to a death much harder to deal with than the actual death itself. This brings challenges though, particularly with wider family not understanding how the death is being processed, how the autistic family member is grieving and thinking that they may appear not to care about the loss of a loved one.

When I was 28 my mum passed away. I remained controlled around other people and would only allow myself to reveal my grief outwardly when I was on my own. When it came to the funeral I really didn't want to go, but not because I didn't want to celebrate my mum's life. In the three weeks between her death and the funeral I had started to process what had happened and what life would be like. Then suddenly, at a point that didn't fit with my own emotional processing, I was expected to attend a massive funeral and relive what happened, how she died and throughout this (and this is the bit I never understood) I was treated by all attendees as being inconsolable. Only I wasn't. I was doing okay at that point. Everyone came up to me and gave me sympathy, cried on my shoulder and told me I would be okay. I was able to cope with being thrown off my course of processing, but many autistic people won't be and it is important to accept that a funeral could be more detrimental to them. Yes, people say we should go "as a sign of respect", but is this really necessary if the person is processing in their own way and is coping okay? Most people wouldn't want anyone at their own funeral if it was going to cause them additional emotional pain on top of what they were already feeling. I didn't attend the scattering of my mother's ashes. I kept some for myself to scatter when the time felt right. Almost 10 years on I haven't done it yet. I'll know when it feels right, and it is not for anyone else to judge.

As a child, Charlotte recalls losing her grandmother and how as an autistic person she processed it:

"My grandmother was the person I loved most as a child. The news she had terminal cancer made me numb and physically sick. I detached myself from the love I had for her and prepared myself for her death. She outlived her prognosis and to my shame I became frustrated at the wait. I would play over in my mind what it would be like and how I would cope. I was on my way home one late May evening, and I knew she had died. I cried a little and when I was told I remained composed and played the piano and moved on as if nothing had happened. To onlookers this may have appeared a cold-hearted response but not a day goes by where I don't think about her, and I will always cherish the happy memories of her. At the same time, something has ended so my brain looks forward and can't dwell."

Funerals for an autistic person can be challenging. There is an expectation of how to show emotion: a conformity that can be bewildering and hard to adhere to.

Showing emotion is difficult for a person with autism and often the outward emotion is different to the actual emotion being experienced by the individual. It is important to remember and inform others that the emotion displayed outwardly isn't necessarily the one they are feeling inside.

In order to attend a funeral successfully there will need to be preparation so there is time for the child to formulate and ask questions and process them.

Discussing death and funerals is a challenge for all parents and also a very individual and personal thing. There will be cultural and maybe religious traditions and views that come into this, and it is important that these are included in what you tell your child. However, they need to be discussed in a way that is clear to your child. Clear language should be used that won't cause additional distress and confusion. Death is an event that has numerous metaphors linked to it and these can cause misunderstandings. You don't want your child to attempt to book a plane ticket up to heaven, for example.

When telling your child that someone has died be clear and factual. Pie was eight when his great grandma died, and I told him that Great Grandma was very old and had died. His response was to say "Bye" and carry on playing. That was it. Even though he saw her frequently he never showed any sign of being upset or confused. For autistic people death gives a finite clarity, which makes it easier to process than for more neurotypical people. If your child is confused about what death actually is, explain that bodies all stop working at some point, whether it is from old age or illness.

If you are taking your child to a funeral make sure that they know what to expect. Tell them where it is and who will be there. It might be easier to tell them it is an event to remember the deceased rather than to call it "N's funeral", as that does sound like the person is going to be there. There is no right or wrong way to deal with grief and if your child does go to a funeral, don't worry if they say something that you think is the wrong thing. It is important that they are able to express their feelings the same way as anyone else.

We would also urge you to think carefully and make sure that attending the funeral is the best option for all concerned.

Religious festivals

For those who belong to a religion, there are also religious festivals. Here we will be using Christmas as an example, but the principles behind our advice are the same for any major religious festival.

Christmas is a challenge for families with autistic children (and adults). Due to the commercialization of Christmas, we see gradual changes everywhere from September through to December. The decorations, music and lights are hard to escape as so many people think they are a beautiful and cheerful addition to our surroundings. They appear at school, at home, in shops and even in hospitals. But what happens if you find all these things a sensory nightmare and just way too overwhelming?

When Kiddo was almost two years old I was so excited at the idea of Christmas. I had such fond memories of decorating with my own mum. We would turn our hallway into a huge grotto full of lights and paper chains. I would sit and stare at the lights on the tree and almost sink into them as my focus made the light expand and fill my vision. I still do the same nowadays only now I realize it is one of my favourite visual stims. I wanted to share the same moments with my son that my mum had given me. I wanted to pass down traditions and have him feel the love and warmth of Christmas that I did as a child.

One afternoon when Kiddo was having a nap, I decorated the hallway in fairy lights and paper chains. Think of that scene in the film *Elf* where Buddy decorates the toy department store with an incredible array of lights and snowflakes and paperchains. That's how my hallway looked. As the lights flashed away I brought Kiddo down from his nap, my heart ready to burst with love and joy. He took one look at the decorated hallway and ran all the way back upstairs to his room and refused to come out. He cried, and as I tried to comfort him I sobbed to myself.

It wasn't the effort I had put in; it wasn't the fact that he didn't like the decorations particularly. It was the realization that my son wouldn't be able to continue the family traditions I held so dearly in my heart. I took the decorations down. Whilst I was removing them, Kiddo came down the stairs and wandered into the living room where I found him standing in front of a bare Christmas tree. I had already assumed that we wouldn't be able to decorate it, but I hadn't got round to packing away the decorations. Kiddo seemed mesmerized by this tree, so I picked up one bauble and hung it on. That was it. Kiddo was in the box grabbing ornaments to hang on the tree. Within a few moments our tree looked like Christmas had thrown up on it and there sat Kiddo, staring up at it in the same way I had stared at ours as a child.

In that moment I had a realization. Why should Kiddo have to follow in the traditions that I had with my mum at Christmas? His brain is wired completely differently; he is never going to feel the same feelings or experience the same experiences as me. It would be unfair to put him through that just for my own enjoyment. My child was autistic and had a different sensory profile to me. It was time to change the traditions. So, we invented our own! We found things about Christmas that Kiddo loved to do. We made biscuits and played Christmas versions of his games and apps on his iPad. We decorated the tree, but we left the lights off. Three years later and he was asking for the lights as long as they weren't flashing. We have created our own unique Christmas and it is more special than ever.

The build up to Christmas is one thing; the day itself is quite another. Family and friends look forward to gathering in groups to celebrate and that alone can create quite a challenge when your family has autistic members. When Pie was very young Charlotte decided that the only way for him to cope with Christmas was to celebrate as an immediate family. Wider friends and family may have been upset about this decision but one of the most important things about being the parent/carer of an autistic child is knowing their needs and how best to support them. For example, if your child attended a large gathering and it was too much for them, it may prevent them from attending a large event again. However, if you take it slowly you are able to build these things up so that they can then accept more in the future. So, with all this in mind, here are some tips to help you before and during Christmas.

Plan early

Whether your Christmas will be filled with family and friends or just a quiet one at home, having an early plan will benefit your child in more ways than one. The less rushing around they witness and the less stress shown, the far more likely they are to remain calm and regulated. Our children feed off our own stress so try to limit that as much as possible.

Only you know what type of Christmas will be the calmest for you and your family. Planning it in advance means extended family or friends won't be disappointed about decisions, changes or boundaries placed nearer the day. Give everyone time to adjust, including your children.

Presents
Not all children want to open presents all in one go. This can seem like a really strange concept to many, but opening presents can send a rush of feelings and emotions through you and can be very dysregulating. For some, it can be hugely anxiety inducing as you don't know what the present will be as you unwrap it. Whilst it can be hard to control what types of presents other people give your children, what you can control is when they open them. Opening a stocking and a large amount of presents all on one day can be really overwhelming. Consider spacing out when your child is allowed to unwrap presents. For example, maybe they open one a day for the month of December, or two or three each day between Christmas and New Year. Most importantly, don't ever force your child to unwrap a present when they don't want to or tell them they are being ungrateful. The idea of opening a gift that you have no knowledge about is not a fun activity for everyone.

Wrapping paper
To wrap or not to wrap? Some people like nothing more than to rip apart a perfectly wrapped present and bow. As mentioned above, this is not always the case. Wrapped presents are a bit of a love it or loathe it concept for autistic children. Some will love the sensory experience of ripping the paper off and will spend more time playing with the paper than the actual present. For others, the anxiety of looking at a wrapped present is way too much, and an unwrapped present is much easier and calmer to process. The type of wrapping paper used is also important. Brightly coloured, sparkly wrapping paper can be great for sensory seekers. For sensory avoiders though, it can be painful to look at and trigger huge overwhelm or possibly meltdowns. Plain brown paper can be a great way to meet in the middle, so consider what type of visual stimulation your child can cope with when accompanied by possible anxiety over opening presents too.

Have a Christmas-free area
Nowadays Christmas decorations flash, sing, move, dance, talk and do pretty much everything except load your dishwasher. Wherever you are

spending your Christmas, whether it be at home or someone else's house, make sure there is an area that is not decorated. Autistic children (and adults) need calm and clear spaces to regulate their senses without any overwhelming lights, movements or sounds. Some children can watch lights and decorations all day, some can't tolerate them at all. Others need to give their senses a break, so a decoration-free zone is essential for when life gets too much over the Christmas period. Perhaps to reduce decorations inside your house you could have more outside instead.

Routine

Even the most organized and planned Christmas will inevitably veer away from your child's daily routine. If routine is essential for your child, keep as many of the core daily events fixed as possible. These include mealtimes, bedtimes, therapy times, quiet times and maybe even homework times if they want. An entire day free from any structure or responsibility can be a really stressful experience, as you have no fixed points in the day to plan around and it takes far more processing. Routine also helps someone to judge the time of day and prepare for the next thing, eventually leading to a calm bedtime routine. Whilst a child may not need their full routine, they may need check-in points so they remain regulated and less anxious. Familiar activities such as watching a favourite TV show or reading a familiar book can be good ways to remind your child that it's just another day and things are safe.

When you are not the Christmas host

Do not assume that whoever is hosting your Christmas understands your child's needs when it comes to the festive season. Our children may adore Christmas and need less support, or they may find it harder and need extra levels of care. Always explain what your child needs, even if your host says they know how to cater for your family. We understand that people may feel awkward about asking for extra, especially if you're not attending your own side of the family.

Explain to your child what happens at Christmas

Your child's ability to remember the Christmas before and how it worked depends not only on chronological age but also their level of understanding. Don't ever assume that they will know what to expect. Where needed, always take the time to explain what this Christmas will look like, who you will see, where you will go and who might visit. Some children will need this early, and others may be better without knowing anything. For some, a visual calendar of events that they can study may be helpful. Others may need a daily timetable each morning so they can know what to expect. Even if your child can usually cope at other times, spontaneous activities may be a little too much to process at Christmas, so be wary of holding the same level of expectation on what your children can and can't do over the festive season. Conversations need to be at the right level of understanding for your child and if the conversation makes them anxious, discuss certain sections of the holiday at separate times so they can regulate in between conversations. If they do have memories from a previous Christmas that are positive, draw on those and use them as reassurance. If they like photos, show them photos from that year. Just don't take it for granted that your child will know what to expect this year.

Controlling sensory experiences

Whilst you won't be able to prevent your child from experiencing all sensory encounters this Christmas, you can help them control their input levels themselves as much as possible. Obviously you can't give your child the switch to turn off all the lights and so on, but consider whether a pair of sunglasses or ear defenders may help them get through the Christmas period. They may not usually need them, but even having the extra option may make them feel safer whilst senses are heightened.

Use an advent calendar as a countdown

Advent calendars can be a great way to help your child gauge how long there is until Christmas Day. Rather than just letting them eat the chocolate or open the figure/toy inside, make a point of talking about how many days are left. If 24 days is too long a countdown period, create your own countdown calendar with fewer days on it. You could even use the advent calendar and the countdown together as another way of showing the child that Christmas Day is getting closer.

Christmas feasting

Many autistic people have self-restricting diets. If your child only eats a few foods, it is unfair to assume they will be able to eat a huge Christmas feast just because it is a national holiday. Always allow them access to the Christmas foods with no pressure, so that they can try new things in a safe environment if they want to. They may wish to try new foods away from the table where there are fewer people watching. Always make sure that there are foods on their plate that they will happily eat. Often children are more likely to try new foods when they are in the habit of eating already so keep the pressure off and don't make them feel bad that you have had to prepare extra food just for them. For some, the Christmas dinner table will be too much to process, and they may find it stressful, especially if there are more people than usual. If they can't cope with sitting at the table to eat, don't force them. They may need down time so they can relax enough to eat. The most important thing is that they actually eat.

Limit guests

Limiting the number of guests doesn't only apply to people who come to your house, it also applies to when you're visiting other people's houses too. Ask in advance who else has been invited and how many people will be there. Explain that surprise guests, or inviting other families to join your party without prior warning, may trigger huge anxiety and may mean you are unable to stay. Do not force your child to stay in an environment that they can't cope with. This is not about other people having the perfect Christmas after all; it's about your child and meeting their needs.

Less is more

For many, the bigger the Christmas the better, and a small Christmas may not be what you had in mind when you started a family. A smaller, low-key successful Christmas is better than a disastrous flamboyant celebration. If you have both autistic and neurotypical children, don't let them miss out. Doing things separately over the Christmas period is not a failure; you're simply meeting everyone's needs. It is not always possible to do everything as a family unit, especially when different neurotypes are involved. With idyllic scenes of families all together plastered as far as the eye can see, you can feel like you're not doing a good job by separating your family for different activities. This isn't true and sometimes the best way to care for a family is to allow people to pick and choose what activities they want to take part in as much as you can. It's perfectly acceptable to ask trusted adults to spend time with your autistic children, as long as your children are comfortable and safe. Perhaps they could have a Christmas treat or an extra present instead of a trip out. Be creative and don't let stereotyped images guilt trip you.

Finally on religious events, many parents can't wait to see their child take centre stage in plays and religious celebrations. There's nothing to say your child can't take part if they want to, but you must think about what they can do if they become uncomfortable or overwhelmed. Give them an exit strategy so that they can be in control as much as possible. Speak with those in positions of authority and explain their needs beforehand. Give them guidance and tell them what your child needs. They probably won't know and will need ideas from you as to how to support you and your family. Pie was never able to participate in nativities when he was younger; however he was delighted when he took part in a Christmas Tableaux at Canterbury Cathedral when he was 13 and a half, and it didn't matter that he was at least five years older than the other participants.

Having always avoided the Christmas build up and finding it overwhelming, Pie has started to get more excited now he is older. This year he has become fascinated with toys that play Christmas songs and is desperate to visit "farmer Christmas" (a term he has used since being able to speak, because Santa is a reindeer farmer!).

What to consider before accepting that big invitation

Although we talk about a few mainstream events in this chapter, the likelihood is that you will be invited to a whole range of celebrations and parties in your lifetime. We want you to feel confident in making the right call about whether your child attending the event is the right decision for them and for your family. So for the rest of this chapter we will talk about the factors you need to consider before accepting that all-important invitation.

Who is the event actually for?

Considering who the event is actually for is something that is so often overlooked. We have already discussed how having a birthday party for your child is so easily planned in a way that the parent thinks it *should* be done and not in a way that your child would actually want it done. Here Charlotte talks about her perceptions of a student social life and how actually people assumed that she wanted the party life:

"So many elements of a social life are created by fads, trends and the expectation of the majority. As a student I was baffled as to why a student would want to go to a nightclub. In my literal world students study, they don't party. Whilst many people would assume that I really missed out on an experience, and what nowadays is considered a rite of passage, by not going clubbing, I would argue that my neurodiversity has in fact enabled me to be more honest with people about what I do or don't want to do. There will of course be autistic individuals who enjoy going out clubbing and will do it because it is what they want to do. However, I know of so many people who will go out and go along with the crowd simply because they do not want to stick out or look different."

What Charlotte touches on here is the importance of asking your child if it is something they actually want to do. It is so easy to get carried away in planning a wonderful day out or surprise for your child because you think they will like it. Or, even more common, because they *should* like it. As I described earlier in the chapter, I am entirely guilty of this and in Kiddo's early years I organized days out and special events that I felt every young child should enjoy. The thing is, this was not necessarily what Kiddo himself would enjoy.

There are obviously times when we have to do things that we don't want to. That is a part of everyone's life, and it should be a part of an autistic child's life too, as it is a valuable lesson to learn. We all need to go to the doctor, or perhaps the hospital. The focus here though is on events that are within your control and making sure you consider who the event is actually for. Is it for your child? If so, you should be looking at the event from your child's point of view and organizing it according to their needs. Check in with yourself and make sure that you are not organizing the event you think they *should* want or like. Remember they may not experience the world in the same way you do. Failing to consider their needs can lead to your child experiencing a harsh sensory and social environment, which may cause trauma and refusal to attend such events in the future. Which brings us to our next point.

What will your child be experiencing at the event?

This is a very important question to ask yourself when it comes to planning and attending big events. In the early stages following a diagnosis, it may not always be clear as you are still learning to read cues from your child. Some autistic children may never be able to attend events, not even in their own home. Learning to accept this is not something that should be dismissed lightly. It is an essential part of parenting a child with additional needs. But why do you need to learn to accept this? Because events can cause such huge sensory overload that the child experiences physical pain.

For someone who experiences noise, light and movement to a much more intense level than the typical person, events can be a sure way to overload the senses and cause physical pain. Personally, at large events I struggle to take part in a conversation when there is background music or lots of other conversations happening at the same time. It makes me feel dizzy and can give me a really painful headache. I find smells I dislike extremely overpowering and feel nauseated and sometimes even gag. Large events can leave me feeling as though I am recovering from a bout of the flu. Sensory overload causes very real physical pain and physical symptoms that can last for days afterwards. This is before we have even mentioned the severe levels of anxiety caused by the idea of socializing with others, which again can cause sweating, stomach ache and panic attacks, which leave you feeling exhausted. So yes, by making your child attend an event you could well be causing them physical as well as mental anguish.

There will also be those who will happily attend an event with seemingly no difficulty but then have a huge meltdown afterwards. It may even occur up to a couple of weeks after the event itself. There will also be a mixture of the two, and you will need to view each event in complete isolation and may not even be able decide until the day itself as to whether it's a good idea for the child to attend.

Events that you organize are always going to be easier when it comes to controlling the environment and making the experience suitable for your child. However, even with the best planning in the world it is essential that you monitor what and how your child is processing the situation; there will always be things that do not go to plan.

What will the after effects of attending the event be?

Events do not just have an effect on an autistic person at the time; the after effects can last several weeks. Events and celebrations take a lot of processing. After Christmas people often talk about feeling low throughout January. For an autistic person this processing can happen after an everyday event, let alone a large one. Imagine there is a threshold within each of us as to how much we can cope with. Sometimes people will cross the threshold during a large event and have a meltdown whilst there. Sometimes they don't quite meet the threshold whilst attending an event, but something minor the next day can tip them over the edge. Parents often look for immediate cues as to why their child is having a meltdown. Sometimes though the trigger is small, like not having any of their favourite biscuits in the cupboard, yet that alone is not what caused them to reach their threshold. The wedding they attended the day before took every ounce of their physical and mental energy, meaning they had absolutely nothing left to deal with the tiniest of problems such as not having the right biscuits. After attending a big event I need to schedule in quiet time on my own with my favourite sensory experiences such as baths and lying in bed. This essentially allows for the negative, pent-up energy to slowly be released from my system. If I can't have this, that pent-up anxiety will come out another way and this is usually far quicker and more extreme in the form of a meltdown. Whichever way a person regulates after an event, it is a huge relief and must be allowed to happen without consequence so that everyday life can continue. However, just because the after effects may appear extreme, it doesn't mean we didn't have a good time at the event itself.

Regulating after an event and processing an event are two different things and often get confused. Regulating, as talked about in the previous paragraph, is when a person allows and helps their body return to a calm physical and clear mental state. Processing involves thinking about the conversations you had, the physical experience resulting from your senses, thinking about moments of joy or moments of anxiety and most of all what the interactions you had with other people actually meant. Processing an event can take hours, weeks or sometimes even years. Both are equally as important.

Even if the event appears to be negative, it doesn't mean that processing it will be. An example of this was when Charlotte took Pie to Disneyland Paris with friends. The event was planned with Pie's needs catered for at every point. It was on the train from London on the way there that Pie started to scream. He did not stop screaming for most of the three-day break. He didn't engage or even eat much. However, on the train home Pie calmed down and started to smile. Naturally everyone assumed it was because they were heading home but when they asked the children if they had had a good time, Pie said he had really enjoyed it! Charlotte was concerned that processing the three days would cause an extended time of distress for Pie, but it was quite the opposite. He looks back on the photos with fond memories.

Of course, the opposite can also be true. We see this with Kiddo often. Whenever he says he wants to leave an event we will immediately go (obviously holidays abroad make it a tad harder to do this!). However, there are many events that he absolutely adores. He loves going for breakfast at our local farm shop and buying vegetables. When we first started going we would stay for up to two hours as he appeared to love it so much. What we very quickly learnt was that even though he adored the experience at the time, the processing and regulating afterwards had a huge impact on him. The noise, the movement and the smells were all things that were almost camouflaged by adrenaline and dopamine from the enjoyment. When that adrenaline and dopamine faded however, he was left with extreme sensory experiences bouncing around his head. The noises were still there, as were the movement and smells. It took him 48 hours to fully recover from a two-hour trip out. So, we started limiting the amount of time he spent at birthday parties or get-togethers. We would always arrive early so he could enjoy some time with the host and it wouldn't launch him towards his threshold as much. From then on it was about learning and watching for signs that he wasn't coping or was beginning to mask. Sometimes we only last 20 minutes at an event, but we leave early as the pain for the next few days for both Kiddo and us just isn't worth it in most conditions. However, this can be difficult to explain to other people.

When you arrive at an event and your child appears to be coping, people will question why you are excusing yourselves early. What people don't realize is that you have begun to notice subtle signs that your child is reaching their threshold. My husband knows that if Kiddo or I blink a certain way, we need to leave immediately. He notices changes in speech (or lack of in my case) and various little tics that we both perform when we are feeling anxious. In order to do this though, you have to be honest with friends and family about just how much support your child may need.

Being honest with friends and family

Easier said than done for many people. Being honest with your nearest and dearest can be nerve-wracking as you don't know what their reaction will be. Sadly there is a huge amount of ignorance around autism, whether it is intentional or not. However, it is vital for your child that you explain their needs and practice doing so. You are your child's main advocate. So often the parent or carer is the person who speaks up for the child and requests adjustments at places like school or medical appointments. Explaining their needs to friends and family is no different; however it does carry far more emotional consequences for the family. Which leads us to our next principle.

What to do when family and friends don't understand

This can be hard, there is no getting away from it. Everybody wants to enthuse about their family life and be proud of their child. One of the challenges faced by parents of children with a diagnosis of autism is that there may have been a period of typical development and no concerns surrounding the child for the first year or two of life. For these parents, explaining the change in need for their child can be one of the biggest challenges surrounding being honest with family and friends. You need to have accepted the situation yourself and certainly early on in your post diagnosis journey this can be hard.

Pie saved Charlotte from this issue. Owing to his gestation, sepsis at birth and complications, she was always left with no illusions from medical staff that Pie would have multiple health conditions and disabilities. She had from a week before his birth to get used to this idea, and for Charlotte the fact that Pie survived was, and still is, a mammoth achievement and has been what has enabled her to fight for him, be his advocate and most of the time remain positive, because however hard it gets, it is easier than not having him. That doesn't mean that she doesn't have difficulty in getting family and friends to understand his needs or see the struggles that other parents go through with this.

We have seen parents who are aware of the needs of their child but feel unable to explain these to others. So often we talk with parents who will openly say things such as, "We haven't yet told the grandparents that X has autism", or will mouth the word autism in the hope that it will somehow eradicate the challenges facing their family. The harsh reality is that to support your child and to get adequate support you will need to be honest. There will be those friends (and family) who fade away but the ones that you are left will be the ones who are going to be there for you no matter what.

Some of the challenges that we face in being honest with friends and family is that there are always those people who will become an expert on parenting and autism and have the answer to every challenge faced by your child. Or even worse, somebody who is in a worse situation or wants to hijack the conversation. It is often worth planning your conversation so that you have a clear idea of what you are going to say or maybe putting it into an email or message so that you know the points that you want to get across can be shared with the person without interruption. When you come to discuss things with them at a later date, you know that the main points will have been expressed and understood.

Remember that just as you need to process information about your child so will your friends and family, so don't expect them to get it right all the time. They may also phrase things in a way that you wouldn't, particularly older people, so again be prepared for this. If you are open and honest with people then you have done everything you can in order to set the foundations for them to have an understanding of your child and family.

It is essential to share with people the highs as well as the lows. It is so easy to become bogged down with the challenges and this can become overwhelming for everyone. Don't only phone or contact a friend or family member when something has gone wrong. They will want to be a part of your child's journey, including the good and the not so good! This will also allow them to be able to plan events that are more tailored to meet the needs of your child, which leads us on to our last principle.

Would a small separate meet-up provide a calmer opportunity to socialize and reduce the after effects?

Whilst we totally get that not everybody prefers socializing in small groups, an autistic child (or adult) may find a smaller meet-up easier to process and regulate from afterwards. There have been numerous times when my husband and I have evaluated the potential impact of the event and decided that it wouldn't be a positive experience for Kiddo. What we do when we make this decision though is offer an alternative, a smaller more intimate meet-up, where Kiddo can enjoy everyone's company (because it isn't that he doesn't want to see people). It means that sensory and social pressures won't disrupt his verbal abilities and that he will be able to communicate with people and enjoy himself. The vast majority of our friends and family completely understand this and have reaped the rewards of accepting we may not attend the main event as a full family, but we are ready and waiting in the wings to see and spend some quality time with them at another point. Obviously this doesn't mean that myself or my husband can't go; it's just about accepting that some events are not right for Kiddo and a smaller meet-up is a positive alternative.

When organizing a smaller event there is something very important you need to make clear though. The people you are meeting up with cannot assume it is okay to invite other people along. Here Charlotte explains how overwhelming it can be for an autistic child or adult when people turn up to an event who you didn't know were coming. As someone who finds this scenario extremely difficult, I resonate with every word of this:

"I had a very good friend when I was in primary and early secondary school, we got on very well. I copied everything she did, and, in my mind, she was cool, incredible and what I aspired to be. On reflection probably a very typical friendship for a girl with autism. However, unlike me she was very sociable and was a twin. When we were about 12, we had agreed to meet up and go swimming at a new swimming pool. I was so excited; I did not get to go out much with friends and I spent what now seems like an age (although in reality it was probably a few days) looking forward to this meet-up.

My grandmother took me to the swimming pool, and I waited, trying to control my excitement for my friend to arrive. Then disaster struck, I could see my friend walking towards the entrance of the leisure centre with her sister and her sister's friend. I got on with her sister and her sister's friend but not in a group and not unplanned. My excitement quickly turned to panic, anger and confusion as my entire afternoon had been ruined. I looked at the clock and had an hour and a half until my grandmother was collecting me and in the days before mobile phones there was option but to get on with it. To anybody who had witnessed me at the event, they would have seen a group of friends having fun whizzing down water flumes, enjoying the wave machine and relaxing on various foam floats. I was struggling, I felt sick, confused and upset and my entire focus was on the poolside clock which at times appeared to be going backwards. My masking cannot have been as good as I thought because the other three kept asking if I was okay, but I could only nod my head as my ability to speak had become impaired and it was all I could manage.

I managed to hold it together as my grandmother and the twins' mother exchanged pleasantries in the leisure centre foyer. As my grandmother and I walked back to her house I hardly spoke as my head was whizzing and spinning in turmoil as she said things like, 'It was nice that there was a group of you!', which did nothing to calm my mood. About two hours after returning home, I had a massive meltdown. It seemed impossible to explain even to my incredible and understanding grandmother what the problem was.

As an adult it might be slightly easier to explain. The change to the original plan was a frustration, but I would not say it had caused the biggest problem. That was the social aspect: having a conversation can be challenging enough, add into the mix the additional background noise of a swimming pool with its large echoing acoustic and then the need to process not what just one person is saying but three was the biggest problem. I still find this today. There are very few occasions where I can cope with speaking on a social level with more than one person. My coping mechanisms have changed and if it gets too much I will leave if I can, but if that is not possible, I must zone out from one person to engage effectively with another.

Whilst some people with autism may cope socializing in small groups better than others, I would always say to start with small steps, follow the lead of your child but remember that it is much better to have small scale meet-ups that work and teach your child to be able to socialize rather than being overly ambitious as that could cause more difficulties in the end."

The point Charlotte makes about only being able to hold a conversation with one other person is so important. I can't even cope when both my son and husband are trying to talk to me, even if by some miracle they take it in turns. Autistic people can find keeping up with conversations where there is more than one other input very overwhelming and anxiety inducing. Personally I feel like the room is spinning and I just need it to stop. I have a couple of groups of friends where I chat easily with two others at the same time, but for 36 years I masked my way through socializing in groups larger than two of us and used alcohol to dull down the anxiety and sensory effects of all the noise.

Children need time to build up these skills. Once they are comfortable socializing with a particular family or person, perhaps suggest slowly increasing it. Throwing them into a huge social situation will not help them though as the feeling of overwhelm will not be easily forgotten and as Charlotte says, will only cause more difficulties further down the line.

CHAPTER RECAP

- When arranging your child's birthday celebration, make sure you keep focussed on what your child can cope with.
- Before accepting an invitation make sure that your child will cope with the event.
- Always explain to hosts that you might need to leave early as this will reduce the pressure on you.
- Explain to your child at an appropriate level before attending an event or celebration what it involves and what might happen.
- Remember that having an autistic child(ren) doesn't mean that you are not able to enjoy events and celebrations. You might just need to make a few changes.

CHAPTER 12

TOILETING AND PERSONAL CARE

I imagine that many of you will have skipped ahead to this chapter, in the hope of some groundbreaking pearls of wisdom that will lead to your child using the toilet. Of all the developmental delays, not using a toilet is a very public one as people can see if you are having to change your child's nappy or pad. This can often come hand in hand with judgemental looks from the general public, or comments from friends and family members listing all the things you should be trying.

We understand first-hand the difficulty of having a child that is delayed in this way; however we are not medical professionals, and it is important that if you need support in this area you seek professional medical advice. What we can do however is to share our own personal experiences and some general information on why toileting can be difficult for an autistic child.

There are several areas of development that will contribute to an autistic child using the toilet a little later than neurotypical children. They may also have periods of time where their toilet training regresses and then improves. Although the timings, methods and reasons for using the toilet (or not) may be different, this doesn't mean they are wrong or failing. Different types of brains work in different ways. Here are some core areas.

Communication

If a child is unable to communicate effectively then they will be unable to let their caregiver know that they need the toilet. This may seem logical, but it can often be overlooked. Even if a child is verbal, remember they may not have developed the communication skills required to talk about their own needs.

Sensory issues

Sensory issues in toileting are vast but typically can include:

- not liking the sensory feeling of going to the toilet
- not liking the sensory feeling of sitting on the toilet
- liking the feeling of a full nappy as this may help them feel grounded
- not liking the sound of a toilet flushing
- not liking the feeling of water when they wash their hands
- impairment to their interoceptive ability may mean that they are unable to know when they need to go to the toilet because their brain is unable to unravel these signals.

Interoception is the sense that helps the brain work out how our bodies are feeling. It is one of the most important factors when toilet training (and is also relevant for girls when they are mensurating). When a neurotypical person needs to go to the toilet, their brain receives a signal to let it know that their bowel or bladder needs to be emptied. Then once they have gone to the toilet, their brain tells them that they have emptied their bowels or bladder. For people with autism, some may receive some of these signals but at the wrong time whilst others may not receive any signal at all. It is important to remember that there can be a delay in sensory development. A five-year-old who has a severe impairment in their interoception receiving no signals to do with toileting may well develop these over time. Occupational therapists are able to devise exercises that may help a person to develop their interoceptive processing.

Focus

Many autistic children become hyper focussed on things that interest them. They become so absorbed that they are unable to interrupt that focus for any reason at all. This includes using the toilet. It can be perceived as laziness, but it is important to realize that moving from task to task can be a huge challenge until either they reach a point where they feel they can leave and return to what they were doing, or the urge to use the toilet becomes too much and they make a desperate dash to the bathroom. In some cases children cannot remove themselves from a task in time, as mentally it is too painful and accidents will occur. Breaking off an activity to go to the toilet means they lose their flow of thought and often it means that they cannot return to the task at all, no matter how much they were enjoying it before they left it. Children need support in these circumstances.

Food and drink

Restrictive diets can cause constipation, which can in turn mean it is harder to toilet train. Fluid intake may also be restricted or limited, and this has an impact on bowel and bladder function.

There will also be very individual reasons why toileting can be a struggle. Co-morbidities both medical and/or developmental can all influence a child's ability to use the toilet. This should not be underestimated or ignored.

Dos and don'ts

Having both encouraged our children to try to use the toilet, with support or independently, there are a few dos and don'ts we can suggest from an autistic adult's point of view:

Do:

✓ Introduce the idea of the toilet. Talk about it and show your children how to use it.

✓ Be patient; it will happen when it happens.

✓ If your child is starting school, make sure the school are aware of the reasons behind delayed toileting and don't just assume you haven't tried at home.

✓ Support and congratulate them for trying, whatever the outcome.

Don't:

✗ Force it; this will only send them backwards.

✗ *No forced enemas.* An enema is often used prior to a medical procedure or if the patient requires it for medical reasons. A forced enema is when the procedure is used as a way of demonstrating to a child their internal feelings before they poo. Professionals can suggest these to "help" a child learn about how they feel so they recognize when they need a poo. For a child who doesn't understand what this is, it will cause trauma. *Always* consult a professional with a qualification in autism or learning disabilities before agreeing to this if there is no valid medical reason.

✗ Never shame the child, for instance by suggesting that their behaviour around toileting is like a baby's.

✗ Never give consequences for getting it wrong; they may not be able to help it or may not be ready.

Support with toileting

Support from professionals on toilet training autistic children varies greatly. In our experience nurses are not always trained in the delays experienced by autistic children and will often approach the delay as they would any neurotypical child. This approach won't work as different brains need different lengths of time to understand toileting. I remember once being told that the bladder and bowel service in the UK was not "a free nappy service" and being scolded for calling. What I actually wanted was advice early on to see if there were any small steps I could be putting in place to help toileting in the long run. I wasn't given any information on autism and toileting at all.

Sometimes as a parent/carer you have to trust your gut (no pun intended) and do what you think is right for your child. I went through the usual steps you would take for a neurotypical child, just to see if they were any help. I wasn't overbearing or stressed about it; I didn't let it rule our lives and I didn't set targets. It became obvious pretty quickly that Kiddo couldn't even process what it was all about. It wasn't the right time, and his development wasn't at the right point, and that's okay. Having accepted a different timeline, another problem became evident: pads and incontinence products.

Kiddo wasn't small for his age, still isn't. He grew out of standard-size nappies available in the supermarket at age four. The cost of Kiddo's incontinence care was so high that extended family stepped in and funded it for well over a year. Having struggled to engage with a bladder and bowel service previously, I tried again and as he was older and had a full-time place at a special needs school I was listened to slightly more. I was told various things, which I've decided I'm not going to write about. I agreed with the plan I was told to follow to get the products my son needed that we as a family couldn't afford. I didn't follow any of that guidance and even informed the school nurse I wouldn't as I felt it was totally inappropriate for an autistic child with major sensory integration challenges and delayed communication. Three years on from that meeting and we have seen super progress with using the toilet. We didn't do anything. He saw us using it, and when he was ready he started using it too. He doesn't use the toilet in all environments, just the ones he chooses. He has times where there is a lot to process in his world and he regresses to using a pad. All children forget some skills whilst they're concentrating on new ones; it's a part of development.

In terms of practical advice when toilet training an autistic child, the best piece of advice we can give you is to be patient. Do not place any negative focus on toilet training. Show your child that you are happy and comfortable using a toilet and if they look interested talk about it. There are plenty of books and videos on using the toilet involving cartoon characters. It may be helpful for them to have access to these, but don't be disappointed if it doesn't result in use of the toilet. Your child may store these images in their head until their body catches up and they're able to work out what needing the toilet feels like.

Nowadays we have a lovely nurse who is supportive and understanding. Sadly though, from what we have heard and experienced, most parents get labelled as lazy when their children don't toilet train in line with others. Keep calm and remember you're doing right by your child. There are some excellent professionals out there with experience in neurodivergence and toileting; you just may not find them in the department you expect to.

Due to complications in his early years, Pie has short gut syndrome and since that day he has been on high doses of strong laxatives. Despite the laxatives he still gets bowel impaction every four to six weeks, which requires a more invasive treatment. When he was four, he was diagnosed with permanent rectal damage as a result of the ongoing bowel issues.

That didn't mean that Charlotte got any different support. She still had to undergo endless rounds of nurse-led toilet training in order for Pie to be supplied with incontinence products. She was selective with the advice that she took. For example, the nurse who had not read any of his notes and recommended she gave him lots of laxative chocolate on top of his already high doses of prescription laxatives was disregarded, as was the one who suggested that if Charlotte put him in pants he would toilet train and the problem would be solved.

Charlotte knew that alongside the organic reason for his problems, Pie's autism played a big part as he was, and is still, unable to know when his pad needs changing. With such little sensory understanding there was little chance that he was going to be toilet trained. Charlotte got very disheartened and like most parents with complex children there is always so much to juggle. When Pie was 12 they finally had a bowel and bladder nurse who understood his needs. Rather than focussing on toilet training she focussed on helping Pie to feel confident and looking at ways to support him.

Once it was agreed that there was no point in pursuing the endless quest of toilet training, the bladder and bowel nurse embarked on ways to boost Pie's confidence around his incontinence. This was mainly down to researching the most appropriate pads for him to wear and letting him try a vast array of options rather than a standard one, which was all that had been offered before. Having the right products made a wealth of difference to his self-esteem and Charlotte didn't spend appointments going over the same things to try that had not worked previously and showed no sign of working in the future because Pie had not changed.

This made so much difference. The guilt of not having a child that would toilet train disappeared and instead Charlotte began to manage a condition and ensure that Pie's needs were met and he was given appropriate support.

Daily personal tasks

Whilst toileting is a milestone which is often talked about by parents, it's rare to hear a parent of a neurotypical child proudly announcing that their child has allowed them to clean their teeth, wash their face or that they managed bath time without a meltdown. For parents of autistic children these daily tasks can be a constant struggle. As with all traits of autism, it is important to remember that there are several potential causes and that these will not always be the same each time.

One reason could be down to planning. As your child is getting ready for school in the morning, they might be focussed on breakfast and having some play time. This may mean that they are unable to focus on things that they perceive to be less important. If they have a set routine then they may find it easier to remember to do everything. Some parents also find timers showing clear time limits for specific activities useful.

The sensory input of most personal care activities is enormous and whilst some of these will stay the same, others may change frequently and be more difficult to prepare for. Having a bath or shower puts a strain on every sense, be it the feel or temperature of the water, the smell of any washing products, the noise of the taps or the way the steam can make the room look different. This can be a difficult obstacle to overcome and will be a very individual one. Charlotte and I know personally that there are times where a shower regulates us, whereas at other times it is completely the opposite. For Charlotte, the droplets of water hitting her skin sometimes feel like hailstones and the noise of the shower is a booming motor similar to a pneumatic drill, which continues hours after the shower is over. For me, the biggest challenge with a shower is all the different temperatures involved. Hot water, cold room, washing hair means my body turns colder without enough water on it. The sharp change from hot to cold is so painful and overwhelming some days that I just can't face it.

Whilst as adults we are able to decide the right time for our showers, it isn't always that easy to interpret the right time for Kiddo or Pie. Whilst Pie is verbal, he is unable to explain what the issue is so it is a matter of needing to see his responses to the idea of a shower and taking things slowly.

Never underestimate the physical pain that personal care can cause. It's important not to tell your child not to fuss or to force them to wash as this sets them up for a future of being afraid of showers and so on. If your child struggles with washing in particular there are some things you can do to help them:

- Ask them what room temperature they prefer as this can make the world of difference.
- Similarly, ask about water temperature. Kiddo finds cool water really soothing but hot water is an absolute no. I'm the complete opposite and like hot water.
- If a bath or shower is too much then consider using a sponge or flannel with soap and drying each area before you wash the next.
- Change your shower head so you can try different water pressures and flow types.
- Bath spa mats can turn baths into jacuzzies, which can change the whole sensory feel of the water.
- Ask your child to check the feel of towels and pick one. Cotton ones feel different to microfibre ones. Towels that have been tumble dried can feel incredibly different to air-dried ones. Maybe a blanket is preferable for them. It doesn't matter as long as they are dry afterwards.
- There are products that don't require water at all and can be used straight on dry skin or hair and then towelled off.
- Make sure the clothes the child wears afterwards provide a calming sensory feel. If your body is overstimulated by washing, then clothing that also overstimulates can tip an autistic person into meltdown.

A major difficulty for most autistic people is teeth cleaning. Again, this can be down to a multitude of reasons. Let's face it, parents and carers spend lots of time telling their children not to put something into their mouth as it is dangerous and then we tell them to put a plastic brush in their mouth. The level of confusion caused by that could be a trigger.

One of the most common challenges with toothbrushing is our old friend sensory processing difficulties. This can be the sensation of a foreign body in the mouth, but the biggest culprit is often toothpaste. It isn't just the flavour of the paste but also the foam it produces. It is often a matter of getting lots of different varieties of paste and turning it into a game when your child is in the right frame of mind. It is important to keep things calm and relaxed and support your child. Let them learn about their personal care at their pace but obviously ensure that there isn't a reason such as pre-existing tooth pain that is adding to their inability to tolerate teeth cleaning.

Whilst it is important to not add additional pressure to your child, this doesn't mean allowing your child to neglect their personal care. Poor personal care does not only have a detriment to their day-to-day life but also can be a reason for other children to be unkind. If you are reading this and you have a young child you may not think this next section is relevant, but please keep reading. Charlotte remembers how quickly Pie went from a child to a now 16-and-a-half-year-old. Just because your child may have a difference in their development, it doesn't mean that puberty doesn't happen.

Puberty

Puberty can be really scary for autistic teenagers. Charlotte remembers her own panic when she was going through puberty. Everyone has that embarrassing situation whilst they adapt to this new phase, but without a doubt autism can make it even harder. One Wednesday evening she realized she had hair on her legs. It looked different, felt different and it had to go. Rather than discussing what was happening she decided to shave her legs with a disposable plastic razor with no water, gel or foam. This was one of her less successful ventures as you can imagine. Her grandmother was very understanding and decided that hair removal cream might be the way forward. On paper it seemed like a good idea; however it requires time keeping and after applying the cream she was distracted and by the time she remembered to remove it her legs were a garish shade of red similar to the colour they were after her shaving attempt.

For autistic girls and women there is the added complication of having periods. Managing periods requires a certain level of interoception, the sense that enables a person to understand their own body's signals and signs. From Charlotte's personal experience this is a nightmare; even if you take away the hormones she finds the practical side is a real challenge. It is something that needs to be managed really carefully and at a level that your child understands and feels comfortable with, revisiting it if they need reassurance.

Make sure that you take adequate time to explain clearly to your child about periods and that it isn't something that is discussed once and then left. As with all things, the autistic brain needs to be reminded of how to manage something and it needs to be regularly revisited. Check in with your daughter every so often and find out if their products are still comfortable and if they are finding any areas challenging. The main difficulties encountered are sensory based. This could be dealing with new odours, getting used to the sensation of blood running, using sanitary products and using public toilets, which may have noisy hand driers and be busy.

When purchasing sanitary products for your child, it is important that you try a variety of products, as it may be that there is a specific brand that your child feels most comfortable with. Adding period pants alongside another product can give your child additional protection, and these are widely available and come in a variety of styles.

Whilst dealing with this multitude of sensations there is also the need to be able to plan. Children must make sure that they have adequate sanitary products with them and plan when to go to the toilet. Some may find it easier to pre-decide when they need to go to the toilet and maybe set a discreet alarm. If your child struggles with interoceptive difficulties then this will be particularly important because they may not be able to interpret their body's signals that this needs to be done.

Supporting your child to deal with discomfort associated with menstruation is important because they may struggle to communicate the pain they are in. It could be a brand-new pain to them and that can be a lot to process as well as potentially frightening. Explaining why periods cause cramps can lessen anxiety around the pain.

It is so important to be patient. Your child may deeply feel the hormonal changes before and during their period, and this can be a struggle. They may become low in mood or be more tired than usual. Remember, difficulty processing feelings can cause erratic behaviour or verbal shutdown. Processing difficulties on top of hormone imbalances can be stressful and at times frightening because you feel so out of sync with your body. Be kind and supportive and never tell them they are being dramatic.

If your child has their period at school, make sure that they have adequate support to deal with it. This could include discreet ways to communicate if they need to go to the toilet or need pain relief or support. If your child is prone to verbal shutdown then communication cards can be a great way to show the need for help or time out without having to talk.

Clothing may need to be considered during your daughter's period. Help your child to select suitable clothing; white trousers or a pale dress may not be their best option. Clothing can feel different on the skin when there is a change in hormones. At times nothing is comfortable and changes to body shape can make items that are usually comfortable extremely uncomfortable overnight. Bras can cause sensory issues on their own, let alone when there is a change in body shape or sensitivity. It may be worth considering shopping for clothes during their period so they can find comfortable clothes that help during menstruation.

Remember that every period is different so your child will need to be prepared that there may be changes in the flow, hormonal sensation and length of each period. This can be quite alarming and a diary of how they felt and when their period started can be really useful as both a way of processing and a reminder that change is normal.

Be open with your child and tell them that every woman has several embarrassing moments with their periods so that when it does happen, they don't feel it has only happened to them.

It is a difficult time for any young person but don't underestimate the magnitude of what your child will be having to deal with when you add autism into the mix.

One of the biggest challenges for Pie with the onset of adolescence was deodorant. Challenge one was getting him to understand why he needed to use it and this is one that to this day is revisited daily. Then came the difficulty of finding one he would tolerate. The answer to this was that there was no one fixed solution because his sensory needs change so frequently. He has sticks, roll ons, salt sticks and a pump one, all of which Pie will tolerate on different days. He does require not only a reminder to use deodorant but also physical assistance with this. Reassurance is key when he feels it is uncomfortable.

With Kiddo being young still, it does cross my mind often how we will deal with puberty when it arrives. You can't always prepare for these things; you never know how your child will deal with them. Whilst I am aware of the challenges that may lie ahead, I don't focus on them too much right now. I just need an awareness of them; after all, knowledge is power. When the time comes we will work together and offer him as many options as he needs. Somehow as parents and carers we have to find a way to not look too far into the future, whilst being prepared at the same time.

CHAPTER RECAP

- Don't be scared to adapt communication levels around this time of heightened anxiety and sensory processing. For example, a verbal child with a high level of understanding may still benefit from using routine boards or communication aids to prompt personal care activities.
- Be aware of known triggers and be sure to avoid them as well as incorporating sensory items that you know your child enjoys.
- If your child has difficulty with motor skills, adapt clothing to make it easier for them. For example, if a child finds it easy to remove their clothing they may be more likely to dress and undress themselves.
- Think outside the box. If your child will happily sit on the toilet whilst having screen time then so be it.
- Make sure that you don't become frustrated with your child. Anxiety can play a big part in toilet training, and you don't want to accidentally add to it.

CHAPTER 13

WORKING WITH PROFESSIONALS

Once you have received your child's diagnosis, this usually isn't the end of working with professionals. How many professionals and which professionals you work with depends upon several factors, including the services available in your area, the presentation of your child's autism and any other co-morbid conditions they have. There will be no definitive list of professionals, but in general they divide into three main areas: health, social care and education. You may find you are working alongside one or more of these teams throughout your child's life. Our experience of working with professionals is based upon the system in England, however ever country will have similar systems even if there are some subtle differences in their precise roles, support offered or terminology.

There are many areas we can talk about with regard to working with professionals. We have broken this chapter down into small sections so you can pop back and refer to a specific area when you need to.

Let's talk about admin

Before we go any further, let's talk about something so many parents and carers will be familiar with before reading this book. Admin. There is no escaping it and it can feel like you're drowning in repetitive diaries, questionnaires, forms and general hell. If someone had asked Charlotte before having Pie what she thought one of the most time-consuming aspects was going to be, admin would not have been on her list. The admin involved in attending appointments, completing pre-appointment forms, writing to education and/or social care teams, completing direct paperwork and so on can at times feel like a full-time occupation. Life can feel very overwhelming, and at times it can feel like admin is preventing you from accessing the support that you need. Nevertheless, you have to find a way to cope with it and there a few things you can do.

- Pre-empt the dreaded words "can you fill out a diary for the next three weeks". Either download or create your own template and as soon as you have your first appointment booked in start recording. You can ask ahead if the professional is going to ask you to do this. I have had professionals refuse to take recorded timetables from me because they are in the wrong format. Do not accept this as a reason to have your data refused. You are the parent, and you have other responsibilities. Should they need the raw data in a different format, they can take responsibility for that.
- Tell the professionals you are struggling to keep up with the admin. They are there to help you. They know what a pain the admin is. Sadly, we live in a world where everything has to be proven with evidence due to people abusing the system. If they can see you are not faking it the chances are that some professionals will find a way to help you. I have had professionals create tables I can stick on my fridge and just tick boxes when Kiddo shows a behaviour or impulse that we genuinely need to gather evidence for medical reasons.
- It is okay to question why admin is needed and why previous figures already collected cannot be used. Professionals may not know that you have already completed this exercise and will not mind you politely asking why. Which leads me on to our next suggestion...
- Do not assume that departments and services talk to each other about you. In our experience, for example, they are hugely over-stretched and underfunded in the UK, and this may be the case where you are too. You will not be at the top of everyone's priority list at the same time. Send notes and records to whoever you think needs them. Make friends with medical secretaries. These people are key in order to keep communication going. They manage diaries and appointments and have a lot more power than you realize. Never underestimate their involvement and how important they are.
- *Make copies of every single thing.* The system is not foolproof and things get lost. It may not be you or your professional's fault, but it will be you who has to re-record the data and there is no getting around that.

- Accept that sometimes the system is bureaucratic to its core. The only way to get what you need is sometimes to give in to this and just get your head down and get on with it.

Tips for working with professionals

Working with professionals can be exhausting, stressful and somewhat confusing. There are however some general rules on how to get the best out of the professionals you work with. First, it is important to understand what the professional you are working with is responsible for to ensure that you are able to utilize their skills and expertise to the maximum. This is often a good question to ask when you first meet a new professional. Gain a clear understanding of what their role is and if you feel anyone is unsure, pop an email over confirming the tasks they are going to help you with.

Mutual respect is crucial between parents and professionals. Professionals have studied hard and often have experience of working with several patients, but as your child's parent you are the expert on them. When Pie was critically ill in hospital, a consultant arrived at his cot with a group of eager medical students. He asked them to tell him why Pie needed surgery. They came up with several reasons but none of them were correct. The consultant looked at them all despairingly, pointed at Charlotte and said, "There is the expert. Forget your textbooks; that there is the most important resource you have." Charlotte felt very embarrassed and certainly didn't feel like the expert. However, nowadays there is no doubt that she is the expert on her son.

Before attending any appointment make sure you are prepared. Ensure that you have background information that may be relevant. If you attend lots of appointments with several different teams, have a timeline and general background information that is easy to print out and this will save you having to repeat yourself too many times. Have a clear objective of what you want to achieve from the appointment and a list of any questions that you think may be useful. This will help you keep the appointment focussed. When you answer questions be factual and concise. Appointment times are limited, and it is important not to get lost in insignificant detail or by being overly emotional. As cathartic as it can feel offloading to professionals, many will not have the time and it isn't always a part of their role.

Take time to listen and ask questions. Whilst it is important that the professional hears what you have to say it is also important that you listen to them. This is especially important if the meeting outcome isn't going the way you had hoped or expected. Whilst sometimes we feel we know what is best for our child, there can be very valid reasons why that is not the case. This can cause disappointment and understand the reasons behind the decisions made can help a child to overcome this. Many a time I have asked why certain medications or therapies are not being considered for Kiddo. As long as the professional making the decision takes the time to explain their reasons, I don't often disagree with their decision. Frequently though, professionals are so stretched in capacity that they don't necessarily take the time to explain their reasoning. This is something you are entitled to know and can calmly and confidently ask for. You never know if that professional has the full picture, whether they haven't been contacted by another team who promised they would, for example. Asking for reasons is a good way to double check a professional has all the information they need. Admin isn't just a nightmare for parents/carers; professionals have a tonne of it too and often things can get missed through human error.

Often following an appointment or a meeting there will be things that need actioning or following up. Make sure you get dates for actions to be completed by and a list of who is responsible for them. Be clear on who is doing what so that you as the parent/carer can make sure you are clear on your own role and who may need following up on for certain tasks.

Parents and professionals working as a team

The relationship between a parent/carer and a professional is complex, essential and integral to getting your child the help they need. As a parent/carer the priority will always and rightly be the wellbeing of your child and family unit. It should be for professionals too, but there will also be budgetary constraints, expected practice, lack of time and large caseloads. Whilst these are valid reasons, there is no reason for accepting a substandard service or for your child not getting the help and support they are entitled to.

As with every relationship it is important to get to know each other, but we don't mean going for a coffee and putting the world to rights! For the professionals it is important that they understand your knowledge and background and have read about your child's presentation. Recently, I met Kiddo's new psychiatrist for the first time. She began by trying to explain to me what ADHD was, suggest I read a book on it and explained that ADHD medication may in fact make Kiddo's autistic traits become more pronounced. Now apart from the rage I felt at the fact my son appearing "more autistic" was a problem of some sort, I felt well and truly patronised as she did not take the time to learn about me or my knowledge on the subject. I made it perfectly clear that I understood the topic and set out to get what I came for, which in this case was medication. This encounter was not positive for me, but it could have been so different. I have a psychology degree, I have ADHD and I run a business explaining ADHD and autism to other parents from an autistic/ADHD point of view. I spent most of that meeting defending my own knowledge rather than talking about my child to gain some mutual respect from the professional and have them understand why I was requesting the medication I was. I was really saddened by it afterwards as I was so willing to learn more. However, the professional had made several assumptions about me and was not open minded, which immediately reduced my trust in them.

By contrast one of Pie's consultants completely understands Charlotte's knowledge and personal experience of autism as well as Pie, and they have a transparent relationship, learning from each other and working together especially when Pie needs a new medication or a change of dose. This approach does not take any more time. On the contrary, often the actual appointments are quick and to the point.

Think before you speak, again another golden rule of any relationship but never more so in this one. During appointments things can be said in the heat of the moment, especially when you're exhausted and have spent hours fighting a system supposedly designed to help you. Either party could simply be thinking out loud, but this can cause anxiety and give the wrong impression. This has happened to me several times. One example came from a professional who has been a godsend to us over the years. I couldn't fault their dedication to our family. When Kiddo was only three the big discussion came up of whether he should be in mainstream or specialist school. As his parents we were of the firm opinion that he needed a specialist placement, as were the mainstream school he was attending at the time. This professional casually said to me on the phone that they didn't think he needed a special school because Kiddo didn't have a learning disability. Now whilst he was right and Kiddo didn't have an intellectual disability, he did have extremely complex needs and a whole range of learning difficulties. That comment sent me into free fall. Why? Because I had spent the previous two years fighting for support, diagnoses, therapies and house alterations. I felt that surely his educational needs were obvious and I wouldn't have to fight. That one innocent, flippant comment hit me like a wave as the anxiety of having to yet again fight, complain and appeal overwhelmed me. I set about planning arguments, researching, getting evidence from the school, the lot. What I didn't realize was that actually that professional didn't have a remit in deciding on education, and when a meeting was held they happily went on the advice of the school and the local education team. I hadn't needed to worry the way I did.

Honesty is the best policy, and it is important for both parties to adhere to this. Even the most well-qualified professional will make mistakes as well as the most well-meaning parents. We could write a book on the mistakes we have both made whilst parenting our boys. Charlotte can remember misunderstanding how to do a dressing change on Pie's central line. She was using the wrong dressings from the pack she had been given and the result was an infection. This was picked up and rectified quickly because Charlotte gave an accurate and honest account of what happened. Similarly, Pie was fed TPN intravenously.[1] This feed is a godsend to seriously ill patients, but the administration of it has to be done exactly right. One night Charlotte received a phone call from the hospital informing her that Pie had been moved to the high dependency unit because he had accidentally been given the TPN at the wrong rate. This could lead to a serious problem; however it was a genuine mistake and the hospital were honest and upfront about this. Charlotte knew that mistakes happened. In contrast there have been other occasions where professionals have not been honest about their mistakes resulting in formal complaints and a breakdown in the relationship.

Guidelines are there to be just that: guidance. Charlotte can remember explaining to Pie's primary school special educational needs coordinator (SENCO) that the phonics teaching method was not working for him. It was too variable, and she knew that learning the shapes of whole words would be far more beneficial for Pie. The teacher spent 20 minutes telling Charlotte about the wonders of phonics and how they benefited every child. Charlotte decided to start to teach Pie using the method she had suggested; it was a very slow task but they got there, and he made considerably more progress using this method.

Don't compare your child to others. Charlotte remembers once being in a meeting in a professional capacity where she heard a colleague comparing the child to others they had worked with and how they had far more severe needs. This added nothing to the meeting at all. You wouldn't go to a shop to buy a dress and have a sales assistant talking to

---

1 TPN is a method of feeding that bypasses the gastrointestinal tract.

you about cars, would you? This is relevant for parents too. Don't worry about other people's children; you have enough to focus on. Once when Pie was in hospital Charlotte was talking to another mother in the coffee room. The mother remarked how poorly her child was but that she was grateful that her child wasn't the one in the incubator opposite, because they looked like ET. Charlotte was shocked that someone would make such a judgement and voice it. What made matters worse was that when she went back into the ward she realized that the child the woman was referring to was Pie!

Safeguarding works both ways. It's an essential part of training for all professionals who work with children. This applies to education, health and social care professionals and is there to keep children and vulnerable people safe. Safeguarding should be at the heart of everything, but it isn't only about ensuring that parents are keeping their children safe. If you have concerns that your child isn't being safeguarded by any professional that works with them, you must report it. Safeguarding doesn't simply deal with abuse; it covers quality of life and dignity of living standards, and if any facet of a child's safeguarding is being put at risk by decisions being made it is important that parents are able to voice these concerns in the same way as we would expect a professional to do.

The roles of professionals

As we have said, the professionals you work with will generally fall into three categories: health, social care and education. We will begin with looking at education because this an area that most parents/carers will have dealings with.

It might be that your child is able to thrive in a mainstream school with minimal support. Even if this is the case, it is important that you make the school aware of your child's diagnosis and have communication with the school's SENCO. This means that the school are obliged to make reasonable adjustments to mitigate some of the challenges of your child's condition. A nice letter at the start of the year or when they join the school can pave the way for open communication about your child's needs.

For children whose needs can only be met without a higher level of support, or who require placement at a specialist provision, there will be more professionals involved. These may not be from your child's school but from the local authority instead. During the assessment period there will be educational psychologists who may assess your child and gather information from their school, from you and your child. There will be placement officers who are responsible for working with you to find a suitable provision, as well as teams of administrators and managers who are working behind the scenes. There are also teams of physio, occupational and speech and language therapists who work for the education department. They provide therapeutic interventions and support in your child's education provision.

You may also see these therapists as part of your child's healthcare team. Health is a team that will be involved during your child's diagnosis, but after diagnosis may have limited input generally if your child is without any co-existing health conditions. The main professionals you would work with are community paediatricians who deal with autism as well as other developmental disabilities. Bowel and bladder nurses work with toileting and problems with the bowel and bladder and can provide your child with incontinence products if required. Dieticians work to support nutrition although this is normally only done if your child is extremely under or overweight or is deficient in certain vitamins or minerals. Physio, occupational and speech and language therapists also work for the health service so it may be that your child receives support via this avenue rather than through their education provision. The availability of mental health services is usually very limited for children with complex health conditions. There may well be several other healthcare professionals involved and these may be based in your local hospital or regional or national specialist centres. If your child has several health conditions, in the UK it is possible to apply for a personal health budget and this can be used to provide additional support for your child.

The final team is social care, and they provide support with daily living and supporting the entire family. Social care can be a difficult team to access as the thresholds for support are high and appear to vary significantly between geographical areas. If your family needs short-term specific support, then it may be appropriate to access Early Help. This is a service that is open to any family regardless of any diagnoses and is not SEND specific. It is worth noting that Early Help can support families in getting a diagnosis. They provide support in several areas, not just social care, and can be a valuable support for the families they work with. For those who need a greater level of support over a longer period of time then referral to disability children's services may be appropriate. One of the outcomes of this assessment may be respite, which is a lifeline for many families with children who have complex and high care needs.

How to get your child referred to a professional

Getting referred to a service is often the hardest struggle for most families, even with a diagnosis. How you go about getting a referral is dependent upon which agency you are working with. Once again this information is based upon the system in the UK, but there will be parallels in your own country.

Before embarking upon any referral to any agency make sure that the service is suitable for the age and the need of your child.

For services that fall under healthcare, if you have a hospital consultant working with you they can do referrals to other healthcare services for you. If you don't have a hospital consultant or you won't be seeing them in the near future, don't panic because your GP is also able to do referrals to other healthcare services. It is worth mentioning that often there are long waiting lists so things tend not to be done instantly, but you can find out waiting time targets. Once you receive an appointment it is often worth phoning the appointment department to see if there are any cancellations as this can speed things up.

Getting additional support at school can be done through the school or independently. Sometimes schools make parents think that any request for assessments needs to be done through them, but this isn't the case. If you feel that your child needs an assessment for an education, health and care plan you can write directly to your local authority requesting the assessment and stating the reasons you are wanting your child assessed. The local authority is required to look into your request within a six-week time frame. If they refuse, there are official complaints procedures. It is often more effective if you can get your child's nursery or school to support your application as this gives it greater validity. However, you are not dependent on them, and if you feel you have enough evidence from other agencies you can apply yourself.

You do not need a diagnosis to apply for an EHC plan. Usually children will be on the waiting list for an appointment or assessment before applying for additional help, but applications are not held back by the wait for a diagnosis.

For social care support there are also various referral routes, but once again you can do it yourself. As we have already said there are clear and high thresholds for social care support, and it is worth checking these out before requesting something that you are not going to qualify for. Social care offer support called short breaks, which has a lower threshold than respite, but still gives the young people opportunities. To find out about short breaks in your area, visit your local authority website.

Getting the team together and keeping them informed

Even teams within the same agency often work quite independently. For example, within healthcare you might have a hospital team, a community team, a specialist team and the Clinical Commissioning Group (CCG) all working with you and this can become quite disjointed. When you add in other agencies, all with various teams, you have a large support mechanism that isn't always working together. Over the past few years Charlotte's family had an increasingly large team working with Pie and whilst they appreciate this support it can appear at times that there is little clarity or sense of direction. Fortunately, Pie's fabulous consultant psychiatrist acknowledged this and called team meetings. These were invaluable not only to discuss what individual agencies were doing but also to make sure that they were all working together to provide Pie with the most effective support.

When you work with professionals from any agency, they will always ask you if you are happy for information to be shared. This is obviously a personal choice, but my answer will always be yes. Despite this there are often times when information isn't shared or fully understood between agencies. As we have already said it can be exhausting repeating information. For the past few years, when there is a big change in Pie's needs, a new diagnosis or a change to support, Charlotte has emailed all the professionals that are working with them. In the long run this reduces your admin time and means that everyone is up to date with the current situation and has all the facts in a clear and concise format that they can refer to at a future date. You can take this approach with any piece of information you feel is relevant to everyone working with your child.

What to do when it goes wrong

There will always be times when mistakes happen or you disagree with the professionals working with your child. This is one of the most exhausting sides of being a parent to a child with additional needs.

There are times when we must appear extremely forceful to ensure professionals listen to us and respect our views. People sometimes are mistaken in thinking I enjoy arguing with professionals. I joke about it with people, but the truth is I hate it. I only want friendly, positive, productive relationships with professionals. I give all professionals a chance to show that this is what they want too. Sadly, in my experience there have only ever been a handful of occasions when, before we talk about anything else, a professional has asked what our views are, how we are feeling, what my knowledge level is and what help we are looking for. All the professionals who have done this are still working with our family to this day. It is important to remember that your role is to be the best advocate for your child that you possibly can. They need you to be the one to learn, take advice and balance out what is in their best interests at every stage of their childhood. Sometimes advocating for your child means you might feel uncomfortable challenging those you are working with. Just remember why you are doing it. This is so your child has the best support and opportunities. Find your assertive side and represent your child. Professionals will respect an assertive advocate, especially as many professionals are parents themselves and understand a parent or carer's love for a child.

On occasions, challenging professionals isn't enough and you have to embark upon formal complaints. Each agency and authority will have their own formal complaints procedure and it is important that you make yourself familiar with what it is so that your complaint can be handled correctly. The formal complaints system exists to catch any genuine problems occurring and make sure they are dealt with properly. They ensure safeguarding is of a high standard, that their service is of a high standard and that families are not being forgotten or slipping through the net. So often I hear of families who wait and wait for years for a service and when they eventually get it, it isn't what they actually need. When I ask if they have complained they say they hate complaining and they can't do it as it makes them so anxious. I understand this as making a complaint can be very anxiety provoking. However, a formal complaint doesn't need to be unnecessarily aggressive or offensive. Maybe you wrote a nice email to your professional the week before saying you aren't happy and never had a response. Put that email into the formal complaint system. Services get audited on their effectiveness at responding to complaints and so ensure that people are responded to. I have put a formal complaint in purely to get a response and get it on the record that my family is being failed. I didn't need to shout: the person dealing with it had nothing to do with my problem. The system is there to help you; don't let it intimidate you by thinking that making a complaint automatically means conflict.

Complaints often come about because the aim of a family does not match up with either the aim of a professional or the aim of a service. The minute a family and professional think the professional is there for different reasons, you risk pulling in different directions and getting nowhere.

Positive stories

As parents of a child with additional needs it is easy to focus on what support you don't have. We could write lots about every disastrous appointment we have attended or every professional who has let our child down, but that wouldn't help you on your journey. There is enough negativity in the media about the state of support and provision. Before we bring this chapter to a close, Charlotte and I want to share our own hugely positive experiences working with some professionals who really did change our lives and get us through some very tough times. Whether you are a neurotypical or autistic parent, parenting autism, ADHD and additional needs in today's world is flipping tough. The problems may not come from inside the home; they may come from ignorance in the outside world or perhaps you just don't know where to start (which may be why you're reading this book). At some point it's likely you will reach out for help, and when you do you make yourself extremely vulnerable. Every now and again a professional hears you. They see you and they step up to help you in ways you never imagined.

Many years ago, I decided to request some advice from a team manager about how a professional was providing support to our family. When I rang the duty desk little did I know that the learning disability nurse who answered the phone that day would be fundamental in helping my family understand Kiddos behaviour, help us learn how to support him and most of all allow him to flourish into the boy he was born to be. There was no trying to change him (or me for that matter) – just a professional who listened, fought for us and understood where we were struggling. She doesn't know this but after our first meeting I cried because I was so relieved to find someone who could not only help us but *wanted* to help us. I don't think she ever fully appreciated her contribution to our family. We wouldn't be where we are without her, and I wouldn't have felt so motivated to keep learning. I've become the parent I was born to be because she pushed me in the right direction and accepted me for who I was.

Then there was Kiddo's enabler. When Kiddo was three years old he started preschool. At that point I genuinely believed that no other person except myself would have the skills, patience and love to care for my child. How wrong I was. Kiddo's one-to-one teaching assistant in preschool developed a bond I didn't think was possible. When he made the switch to special school she became his enabler, and we never let her go. She has grown along with Kiddo and us and is like a second mum to our child. I wouldn't be where I am today without her. Kiddo certainly wouldn't. She kept us laughing when we didn't think it possible; she kept me motivated to keep fighting for his needs.

There are several other people I would love to talk about: our incredible autism speech therapist, our community care worker who was always willing to put himself on the record and fight for financial support for respite and so many teachers at Kiddo's school.

When this team are sitting around a table and their sole focus is Kiddo, I see what the system should be, how it should work and what it should do.

If it were not for the skills and dedication of the first team of professionals who worked with Pie at his neonatal unit, there would be no Pie. They taught Charlotte what a good team should look like. They were honest and they listened to the parents' wishes. They were caring not just to the babies but holistically to the whole family unit. Pie has always had teams of professionals working with him but over the years as his needs have become more complex it is the support and work of a few individuals that stand out.

Pie's consultant psychiatrist is a skilled clinician who, from the moment she first met Pie, impressed Charlotte with her understanding, caring attitude and dedication. She ensured that other professionals listened, were held accountable and worked as a team whilst looking at the impact Pie's challenges had on the whole family. When Pie's needs were becoming even more complex, she successfully referred him to the National Centre for Complex Autism and Learning Difficulties.

Pie's personal health budget nurse has also gone above and beyond ensuring that referrals are made and outstanding items are followed up and resolved. Pie's enabler understands him in a way that fills Charlotte with awe. Pie values their friendship and the respectful and dignified way she carries out her work. Pie's tutor has worked with him for the past five years. She is always finding engaging ways to teach him and has a unique ability to differentiate and work on a minute-by-minute basis adapting to Pie's needs.

Whilst it is important to make people know when things are not working as you feel they should, don't forget to tell them when they are going well or when professionals are going above and beyond. They work in a highly stressful and pressurized environment and a "thank you" can mean so much.

And remember – even if personalities clash sometimes or you have to wait to be seen by a specialist – there are some incredible professionals out there. A good relationship with a professional is worth fighting for.

CHAPTER RECAP

- Be clear about your requirements when working with a professional team.
- Don't be scared to ask a question.
- Make notes if this will help you.
- Arrive for appointments with plenty of time so you are in a clear and relaxed frame of mind.
- Follow up appointments with an email saying what worked well and what didn't.

CHAPTER 14

SELF-CARE AS A PARENT/CARER

Self-care is a concept that can be misunderstood. People have visions of being tucked up in a blanket, eating chocolate and watching TV. Of course, sometimes this is just what the doctor ordered; however self-care for parents and carers is so much more. Parents expressing their exhaustion and stress can also be met with controversy as there is an argument that our children experience much worse in their daily lives than we do. It's important to understand that as a parent the stress we experience is hugely different to the stress our children experience, especially if you are a neurotypical parent and your child is autistic. However, that doesn't mean that the feelings you encounter are any less valid. They are just different.

Our acknowledgment of our stress as parents of autistic children can be seen as complaining that our lives are dreadful and suggest that our children are not our focus. It's a difficult balance to strike, but hopefully this chapter will help with ideas on how to look after yourself, which is essential. You cannot care for a child if you do not have energy or patience. The right level of self-care is essential; it is not a luxury you can afford to forego.

Self-care vs self-soothing

So, what do we mean when we say "self-care"? One of the biggest confusions we see frequently is between self-care and self-soothing. Many people believe that self-care is about flopping down on the sofa when you have no energy left, popping on your favourite film and shutting out the external world for a couple of hours. This is actually a form of self-soothing. There are many definitions online for self-soothing in adults, but I particularly liked this one: "Self-soothing means calming your own anxiety and fears when negative triggers tip you over into emotional acting".[1]

It's when you get to that point when you can't carry on acting in a manner that doesn't involve immediate emotional reactions. Your body essentially functions in a state of fight or flight because your levels of adrenaline are far too high. To counter this you need to take some time for yourself, allow yourself time off from chores whilst the kids are at school and so on. Don't be fooled into thinking this is self-care though. Self-care must be sustainable and continuous in everyday life. If your self-care is effective you will rarely reach the point of needing to self-soothe.

Some parents live in a cycle of ignoring their own needs for the majority of the time, crashing from stress and a lack of energy and self-soothing until they can start again. I can actually hear my husband laughing as he reads this because I'm no better at this than most people, although I have been able to regulate my energy levels considerably since starting ADHD medication. Make sure you consider underlying health conditions as well as whether you are just tired. Sadly, many carers ignore signs of poor health, but we shall return to this later.

What is self-care?

So if TV and chocolate is self-soothing, what is self-care? I'm sure many of you have been told to be kind to yourself; it's a sentence I hear regularly. It wasn't until Kiddo was probably five or six that I stopped and really thought about what being kind to myself meant. In essence it was doing things to make myself feel better and happier. I looked at the activities I was doing to try to achieve this. I was shopping (for me it's a dopamine hit), taking baths, eating the food I wanted and forcing myself to sit and watch TV. But if I was taking all this time for me, why didn't I feel any better? It was then that I realized that true self-care starts by coming from within you. It's a permission that you need to give yourself. I could take all the hot baths I wanted, but what was the point if my inner self was constantly telling me that I should be doing other things? Was criticizing me for being selfish? Was telling me that I had a beautiful child and had no right to feel stressed, angry or upset? I was getting out of the bath feeling worse than when I got in. So what was the point? I stopped doing anything for myself because ultimately it all made me feel worse.

1   Counselling Directory, 2017

This situation won't be true for all parents and carers. The needs of our children vary hugely, and every family has different circumstances to contend with. Some will find my situation very familiar; many won't have ever reached that point (I hope). A part of self-care is about acknowledging your feelings and allowing yourself to feel them. Sure, other people may not feel the same way or agree with how you feel, but they're not you. No one can tell another person how to feel. However, how you act on those feelings is a different matter.

I know many people suppress their feelings as they don't feel they have time to deal with them. Perhaps they're just not important right now. An effective step towards long-term, sustainable self-care is finding a safe environment to explore your feelings and accept them. For me this was cognitive behavioural therapy. For others it's a support group, friend or family member. Many people use social media for this, but it's important to be aware that using a public forum places you at risk of criticism and misunderstanding and is not necessarily a "safe space", so use with caution. However you do it, processing emotion is a hugely important part of self-care.

Self-talk often goes unnoticed by many people. It's easy to carry on throughout the day listening to yourself without asking how you would react if someone else said those things to you. If you had to process those thoughts as words physically spoken to you, how would they make you feel? Would you continue spending time with the person who said those things to you? If the answer is no, then why are you talking to yourself that way? I've met so many parents/carers who care so deeply about their children that they are their own biggest critics. I don't think I have ever met a parent who hasn't second guessed themselves, regretted a decision they made or hated themselves for putting their child through something that in hindsight they shouldn't have done. The thing is, we are human. Neurotypical or autistic, we are all going to make mistakes. Even the best, most understanding, most experienced parent will not get it right 100 per cent of the time. And that's okay. It's how you move forward and learn from the mistakes that counts. A mistake is an experience; it's knowledge and a lot of the time it can be used to help others. Charlotte and I did not write this book based on a lifetime of perfect parenting. Quite the opposite in fact! Over the years though we have realized that getting it wrong is actually an incredible opportunity. Look at the situation, look at where it went wrong and think about how you can do things differently next time. Not taking the time to evaluate parenting practices is something that can be changed. Just take a few minutes to consider what you learnt.

There is no guilt in that, only positive parenting. The self-criticism has no place once you have evaluated the situation in question. It will only lead to burnout and self-soothing.

Sometimes it can be really hard to take advice on your own child, especially when they're not neurotypical and they're exceptionally good at masking. You can feel like no one else in the world understands your child except you. For the most part this might be true, but what we often see happen is parents become too afraid to take advice. They block off any other opinions to the point they can't actually make space in their brain for new ideas, even when they come from the most exceptional professionals. We understand that this is a survival mechanism and for so many parents it's the only way they feel they can keep their child safe from the neurotypical world. When you have seen your child go through traumatic situations and take days, weeks or even months to recover, you will do anything to stop it from happening again. The danger with this is that you can end up closing yourself off from help and support, and as a parent/carer this is something that you need consistently in order to keep your self-care going. We aren't saying that you have to do what people say; far from it. Just try not to close yourself off from conversations that you and your child may benefit from. The conversation you have with someone else will not damage your child. You are still in charge of that; you have the right to argue why something should not go ahead and your concerns about it. However, these conversations also serve as an excellent way to help you work through your thoughts and decisions when you find someone who listens to your arguments. It is also fine to write down your reasons for certain decisions. You will be asked to explain these time and time again, and it can be exhausting to reiterate the same points over and over. Keep a written copy, email it out to people after meetings or take printed copies with you and tell people to read it. Having to hold all that information in your head takes up space you need to keep yourself happy and healthy. Write it down. No one has the right to demand verbal communication from you.

In the same way blocking out other opinions can sometimes be less helpful, so can refusing to ask for help. I know that so many times in the past when I have had to explain why I will not be acting on someone's advice, it can then make it seem like it's almost impossible to ask for help. It is always okay to ask for help. Whether you come across as the most capable parent/carer in the world or whether you have argued with every professional you have ever worked with, this should never become a barrier to asking for help. This may seem like a strange point to include in a self-care chapter, but it is so important. If you don't feel you can ask for help it contributes to a feeling of isolation, hopelessness and overwhelm. These are feelings that if left unchecked can lead to depression and anxiety. We understand that often people want to ask for help but have nowhere to turn. For this, you must start at the very beginning. Always have the phone number of the main switchboard for disabled children's services in your area. Tell them you need help. Email them and say the same. It can seem like asking for help is an impossible act to fulfil, however it's not your job to find the right person. Just keep asking until the service finds the right person. Yes, you will need to chase; the bottom line is don't let yourself become closed off. Self-care includes sharing the load. You never have to do anything you feel uncomfortable with as a parent.

With asking for help comes the risk of people not understanding your situation. Developing a thick skin does not happen overnight. Over the years of blogging, I have spoken with parents who are brand new to being their child's advocate and those who have children who have transitioned to adult services and are experts. The difference in confidence is often astounding. Parents/carers who have been working with these services for a long time aren't more confident because they're naturally that way. They've been advocating for their children for years. Allowing criticism and misunderstanding to just bounce off you and not affect your day, week or month is an acquired skill and one that as you go through this parenting journey you will build up. Experience brings confidence. If you're just starting out learning about autism then maybe comments deeply affect you right now. This is simply another chance to learn. To look back and evaluate. It's not an easy thing to do; Charlotte and I know this. I've had comments made that have cut through me like a knife. Some stayed with me for years. This is normal and something that can be worked on as part of your self-care. Look at why these comments upset you, look at who said them and why. It's all about finding peace in the fact that no matter how you parent and what you do, an onlooker (professional or not) will take things at face value. Over time you will learn how to process this in a way that doesn't result in self-criticism.

Although we have a separate chapter on professionals, we want to just briefly talk about it here as well. There will always be times when professionals disagree with your opinion. This doesn't mean to say that they will be rude or aggressive about it; it's more likely they could miss something you have been working exceptionally hard on or not see why you have made a change and question it. This is something it took me a long time to work out and come to terms with, but once I accepted it my life was genuinely easier as parent/carer. Professionals are human like us and will make mistakes. They are overworked and are trying to reach an impossible number of families. There will be days when they have a bad day or make an assumption. How you react to that is up to you.

When I was first starting out, my expectations of professionals were seriously high. Over the years I have learnt to prioritize what I chase and complain about. Again this might sound like a strange point to make on self-care, but it really was life changing for me and gave my brain space to start engaging with healthy activities. Spending your life arguing and complaining with professionals will not bring you happiness. Of course, there are times when you have to fight and the cause is justified. There are things I will not let drop with Kiddo. However, whereas I used to waste my energy demanding phone calls with professionals, asking where various reports were and reacting emotionally to flippant remarks, I now create space for myself by selecting which cause to fight at any one time. Sure, maybe there are two or three things I have to push for and fight, but never more than that. Obviously when you have a child with extremely complex needs it is more likely you will have several issues of equal importance you have to keep on top of. That's hard, and in that case we recommend the rest of your self-care is really prioritized. The best sentence I started using a couple of years ago was, "That's the next fight." I used to think that if I hit all the fights in one go I would reach a point where everything was in equilibrium. That finally everything would be ticking along as it should, and I could relax. The world is a constantly changing place, your child is a constantly changing person. You never know when a new situation will arise and you will need to pursue it. To make sure you always have enough fuel in your tank, to make sure you are always ready to step up for your child, you have to create some small pockets in your life for you. I'm not saying we should all be off on weekends away every week, I'm saying that that cup of tea thinking about something completely different is okay. This is a continuous journey. There will be periods of calm and periods when it's time to change things up a bit. No child can be expected to stay still their whole life. You need to be prepared for change at the last minute, and to do that you cannot fill your head with problems and fights and complaints that actually may not be a priority right now. Pick the important stuff; letting less important stuff sit on the back burner for a while doesn't make you a lazy parent or an incapable one. It makes you a responsible one.

Self-care out in the world

We have talked a lot about the self-care that needs to come from inside you. Of course, there are activities in the wider world that if you are able to engage in will also benefit you greatly. Again though, these might not be what you think. But first, let's cover the ones you may have heard of.

It's an all-too-common situation that parents and carers lose time to work on things they feel passionately about. Of course you do; there are only so many hours in a day and after all, we chose to become parents! Very often parent/carers lose the times that most families would see as recovery time. Perhaps your children don't go to bed at 7 p.m.; maybe you don't get a couple of hours with your partner in the evenings. When you are parenting a child with significant additional needs, finding time for yourself is often a challenge. With the time you do have, it's about choices. Now of course it would be unreasonable to expect you to spend all your free time (no matter how small that is) taking part in art and craft, music, writing, exercise or whatever you used to do before you became a parent. There are jobs to do at home, bills to pay and laundry to do. It's an unreasonable expectation for people to just drop those things in favour of hobbies. What you can do though is ask exactly how many of those jobs are essential. It's not easy to change standards you have held for many years of your life and for many people having a clean house is in fact extremely important when it comes to their mental health. When you become a parent/carer, you almost need to reprogram your priorities and re-evaluate how much happiness a clean and tidy house will bring you now your life has changed. Will doing all the chores perfectly bring you the same level of happiness if it means that all your free time is spent doing it? Perhaps it will; many people get huge enjoyment from it! But what if it doesn't? If you use your time to tidy everything perfectly only to enjoy it for a couple of hours before it's messy again, it could be time to rethink things. What is going to make you feel good? What is going to help you feel refreshed, energized and ready to care for your child? What is going to put you in the best frame of mind so that your child is going to see you at your very best? It's a vicious cycle of spending time doing the things you *think* you need to do, only to be exhausted and shattered when your child is suddenly returned to your care. I can remember a time where I tried to squeeze so much into the school day that by the time Kiddo came home I was beyond exhausted. He didn't get the best of me, the part that I so desperately wanted to give him. This led to me not parenting to the standard I wanted, criticizing myself, and before I knew it I was back in that cycle of burnout and self-soothing. Ask yourself: what will help you feel the best you can for when your break is over?

The subject of guilt from taking time for yourself has been a prominent topic in the conversations we have had with parents over the years. Parents and carers can often live under the illusion that time spent socializing or doing something they enjoy is selfish. No. It isn't. Actually it's the complete opposite; it's very necessary for the reasons just listed. How are you serving your child by being tired, grumpy or depressed? You're not.

Spending time doing the things you love is not something you need to ask permission for. There is a balance of course and only you can know when you're not giving enough to your child. But taking time to go for a coffee with a friend when the housework needs doing is not selfish. It's essential for your whole family.

As well as time for hobbies and passions, another thing that can drastically reduce is time for paid employment. Some parents/carers have to make the agonizing decision about whether to give up work and become a full-time carer. There is the obvious financial pressure involved with this decision and that can cause huge amounts of stress. However, there is also the pressure of losing a career that's taken years to build up, losing adult socializing and losing a job you love. This decision is one that so many parents/carers have contacted both Charlotte and I about throughout the years.

The choice was made for me. I was a childminder and Kiddo couldn't cope with people coming and going all the time. It was way too distressing for him. I also had so many appointments I physically couldn't work. Letters were flying through the door for hospital appointments, therapies and assessments. I was self-employed so didn't get holiday pay. Financially the only way I could get to everything Kiddo needed was to give up work and claim benefits. I never thought I would ever be a person on benefits. I never had any problem with those who needed them, I just didn't foresee a life change so drastic that I would need to give up work. That concept alone was enough to cause me huge stress. Apart from anything else, I just didn't know how to not work!

Charlotte also had no choice and for many years didn't work because Pie was an inpatient. Again, circumstances made this decision for her, and once Pie was settled with a tutor programme and respite, Charlotte returned to part-time teaching. I knew that with Kiddo's needs it was highly unlikely I would find an employer who could be flexible enough for me to leave at a moment's notice, keep hospital appointments and make sure Kiddo felt stable and secure in life. So I began to work for myself.

At first it was volunteering and a blog online, then opportunities began to arise when I really didn't think they would.

So, how do you make this decision? First, remove any guilt from the equation. The minute you start feeling guilty for not working or not being a good enough parent/carer you find yourself immersed in confusion and self-criticism. You didn't know this was going to be the situation you would end up in; you can't see into the future. Give yourself a break. So often I hear the words, "I can't afford to do it." That is not always a good enough reason to not give up work. Why? Because most people haven't been to their local Citizens Advice Bureau, they haven't got advice on how to reduce living costs, they haven't considered the savings on commuting and childcare. Yes, you may need to make sacrifices. The question is whether those sacrifices are worth it. There will be time to re-evaluate your position; no situation is forever. Don't panic that employers won't like the gap on your CV; there won't be a gap. Just a date range that says full-time carer to a disabled child. I'm telling you: I think I learnt more from the four or five years I spent "not working" than I ever did in a career. Carers Allowance is a tax-deductible benefit in the UK for a reason, because caring is bloody hard work, and you get given National Insurance contributions by the Government.

Many people say they can't cope without their job. This is understandable as for so many people it feels like a break from caring that you don't need to feel guilty about. For others it's a way to keep their mental health in good check by exercising their brain in different ways. I understand these reasons; they were reasons for me to stay in employment too. Sometimes though, you have to make a decision for your child and family that involves a huge amount of self-sacrifice. Ask yourself how your child will come through this difficult phase if you aren't around. Maybe you have family members who can help. Perhaps there is a new system you can set up to help with childcare. If you do continue to work, you must tell your employer the truth about what is happening at home. You will need their support if you are to continue working without it causing you even more stress. You're not a lazy person for giving up work to care, you're a dedicated parent. You're not a rubbish parent for continuing to work; you know you need it so you can remain a strong support for your child. All we can advise is that you check the facts before you make a decision, as it may be possible to make changes you had never considered.

The world can become very small when you're a carer, especially if your child struggles with leaving the house. The wider world is a place full of sensory overload and often children choose to retreat to their safe space at home to rest and recuperate. They need this and must be supported in this; however maybe this isn't what you need. Never underestimate what going out into public places by yourself can do for your health. Kiddo was school age before I could start to do this. I didn't go out for a while because I didn't have anyone to meet for coffee. One day I needed to go to town to pick up a few bits. Just walking through the high street, talking to other adults and browsing the shops recharged me in a way I could never have imagined. Even as an autistic adult (not yet professionally diagnosed) who quite often can't stand crowds, I recharged in a way I didn't know I could by doing this. I had to remind myself that the world was still out there. That other people continued to exist in what seemed like a parallel universe. It was a strange experience, but sometimes it can refill your cup in a way you might never have considered. Of course this won't be right for everyone, but ask yourself if you need to remember what the world is like outside of your front door.

The bottom line is, self-care is important. It is as important as everyone says it is, even those people who are not in your position who constantly remind you to look after yourself. The difference for parent/carers is *what* self-care is. Make sure you are caring for yourself in the right way. After all, who has time for a flipping bubble bath?!

CHAPTER RECAP

- Allow yourself to be aware of your feelings and know that they are okay and valid.
- Don't be overly critical of your parenting.
- Accept help and advice.
- Allow yourself time to be yourself.
- Don't neglect your own health.

CHAPTER 15

ADVICE TO OURSELVES

To end the book, Charlotte and I thought about what we would have said if we had the chance to go back and talk to ourselves whilst we were pregnant. Then we realized that, owing to our diagnoses, our advice may have been very different to what a neurotypical parent would have told themselves. This chapter is split into two sections, the first being tips from Charlotte and I and the second coming from my blog followers on *The Autism & ADHD Diaries*. Their honesty about what they would have done differently is so raw, honest and refreshing. We hope it helps those of you reading this who are just at the beginning of learning about autism.

What Charlotte and I would have said to ourselves
Keep calm and don't make quick decisions
When the system is stretched and resources are rare, you may feel like at times you need to make quick decisions. When you have ADHD you are even more likely to do this, making snap decisions that are impulsive and perhaps not as considered as they should be. When you need to make a decision, ask for the deadline. Even if you only have an hour, secure a time slot when you can think and then take the next step. Do not be rushed; you have the right to be able to make considered choices when it comes to your child.

Be as flexible as possible – what works one day might not work another
This was a hard one to come to terms with, especially for me. My brain likes ordered systems and processes that have a history of being success-ful. But for an autistic child, each day brings different stresses, sensory challenges and processing complications. You won't always know why, but something that has worked once may not work on any other day.

It could be that something you did the day before or something that is due to happen the next day is causing your child to dysregulate. Be compassionate and supportive. Do not be disappointed if a routine or regulatory activity that has worked before suddenly stops being effective.

Keep a diary of relevant behaviours and symptoms

Both Charlotte and I learnt this very early on, but we still had a significant amount of time where we would wait for an appointment, be so relieved to reach the top of the waiting list and then be told to go away and spend at least another month filling in diaries. Be proactive and do it first. You may need to record food eaten, sleep had or behaviour. This can help show sensory challenges and also that your parenting is not at fault. Build the evidence, keep it and use it. Stick sheets on your fridge with tick boxes for different times and behaviours. Make notes on your phone. Spotting emerging patterns will help you and your child so much.

Learn as much as possible about your child's diagnosis

Knowledge is power, which is probably why you're reading this book. If your child is diagnosed autistic, this doesn't mean they will be similar to any other autistic person. Yes, we suggest you research and learn about autism and/or ADHD, but more importantly learn about *your child's* autism and/or ADHD. What works for them? What doesn't work? You will need to become the expert on your child and be able to feed back that information to anyone who needs it.

Enjoy every achievement

Whilst some days will be a struggle (as for all parents), there will be the most beautiful moments too if you let yourself see them, like the day Kiddo went and found his shoes when I asked him to. To everyone else such events may seem small, but to us they are so big. You know what the challenges are for your child. When they beat one or achieve it, make sure you celebrate with them and sod anyone else who thinks it's a silly achievement to make a fuss over. Take time to be yourself.

This is easier said than done but so important. It can be really challenging to find childcare where your child can cope. If you can, make sure that you spend time doing something you love. There will always be housework. There will always be jobs that need doing. But parenting a child in a world that's not built for them can take every second of your time and attention. Use any free time for you first. Then consider your housework and so on. Don't forget those hobbies, don't ignore your interests. Even if they have to be put on hold for a while, don't let them gather dust in the corner for too long. When Kiddo finally started school I was lost (after about three weeks of solid sleep). I couldn't remember who I was. If you can, try not to forget yourself. You may be a parent/carer, but you are still you.

Allow people to help

There is nothing wrong with admitting you're tired and struggling. It doesn't make you a failure or weak. It will actually make you stronger and a much better parent in the long run because you start to see the benefits of rest if you can get them. If people can't help with your child then get them in to do housework, ask them to do your shopping. It's not only childcare that people can help with. Reaching out is a strength, not a weakness.

Don't ever allow a diagnosis to become an excuse

Looking back, we aren't sure if we did this or that others did. Either way, being given a formal diagnosis of anything can give you huge amounts of help. It can also become a reason not to try, not to push your child just a tiny bit further, not to show them what they are capable of. Being autistic (and/or having ADHD) can sometimes make the world a more challenging place. However, there are changes that can be made to support you or your child. It's very easy to hide behind a diagnosis and say, "My child won't cope with that" because you are protecting them. Sometimes this will be the right course of action. Sometimes it could prevent your child from learning something about themselves that could increase their self-esteem hugely. Gently pushing your child in a supportive and safe environment can be the key to unlocking their confidence. Don't let a diagnosis be an excuse; our children are capable of amazing things.

Educate close family and friends

As a parent of an autistic child, you won't only learn a huge amount, you will see the world from the most amazing perspective. A perspective many will never know is possible. Tell people about it. Tell them why certain things are a struggle, why your child finds different things interesting. The more we educate the wider world, the more autism friendly it becomes. You need your friends and family to be accepting of your child's needs, but they will struggle to do that unless they know why. And if you don't have time, give them this book and ask them to read it.

Challenge professionals if you need to

It is absolutely okay to politely challenge professionals and their view-points. We are all learning all the time, especially about your child. There will be things professionals haven't seen at home. There will be information about autism they're perhaps not yet familiar with. No professional will ever purposefully make a bad decision, but it's up to us to be the best advocate we can for our children. Don't ever stay quiet; if something is nagging you or you feel something is wrong then say. If you don't want to say it verbally, send an email after the meeting. Get your viewpoint down in writing and be the fighter your child needs you to be.

Advice from other parents/carers of autistic children

The following points are taken from my blog followers. It was an emotional read looking through all the responses. Parents had clearly come on such an incredible journey and had so much they wanted to share with those just starting it. I haven't directly quoted all the points and have combined some together. Thank you so much to everyone who gave the time to really think about what they would have told themselves.

- Throw any thoughts of traditional parenting out the window and embrace the difference in your child.
- Listen to your gut instincts. You know your child more than anyone else.
- Find your tribe and spend time with families like yours. Laugh and cry, support each other and support each other's children. We all want the same thing: to help our children grow in a happy and safe environment.
- Stop fighting battles you and your family don't feel are important, even if everyone else is telling you it matters. It doesn't matter where they eat as long as they eat. It doesn't matter if they wear the same outfit every day. Your priorities will be different and that's okay.
- It's our responsibility to be our child's voice. Ask people to change and adapt the rules to accommodate your child because it's not always the case that this will happen automatically.
- Be more understanding. Step back and try to put yourself in your child's shoes. Tell yourself to be a better parent.
- If you've met one person with autism, you've met one person with autism.

- Don't buy toys you think your child *should* want. Buy what they're actually interested in.
- Learn to let others help. It's a strength not a weakness.
- Be prepared for your parenting to be judged. Other's will not understand your child's needs.
- Don't be frightened of a diagnosis, it opens so many doors.
- Don't overly push your children. Let them show you when they're ready to grow and progress.
- Work in partnership with your child, and treat them as you would want to be treated.
- Don't take their behaviour personally. You are their safe person.
- The faster you drop preconceived ideas and expectations, the easier it is to embrace and celebrate all that your child is.
- Be flexible in your expectations as a parent; be prepared for things not to go to plan.
- Use what you have learnt to educate your family and friends.
- Remember, your child doesn't need fixing.

To be able to talk to someone who has already been through something you're experiencing is the most valuable way to learn. After all, hindsight is 20/20. We hope these points give you some guidance and help you realize that you are not alone: we are all there with you.

References

ADDitude Editors (2022, April 15) *6 Essential, Natural Supplements for ADHD*. ADDitude. Accessed on 04/05/2022 at www.additudemag. com/slideshows/adhd-supplements-fish-oil-zinc-iron.

APA (2013) *Diagnostic and Statistical Manual of Mental Disorders (DSM-5)*. Arlington, VA: American Psychological Association.

Cookman, D. (2018, January 19) *How does Australia's migration system deal with disability?* SHG. Accessed on 04/05/2022 at https://www.shglawyers. com.au/how-does-australias-migration-system-deal-with-disability.

Counselling Directory (2017, May 17) *6 ways to self-soothe when you're feeling rattled*. Counselling Directory. Accessedon 04/05/2022 at www.counselling-directory.org.uk/memberarticles/6-ways-to-self-soothe-when-youre-feeling-rattled.

Mencap (n.d.) *Learning difficulties*. Mencap. Accessed on 04/05/2022 at www. mencap.org.uk/learning-disability-explained/learning-difficulties.

Millar, S. (1973) *The Psychology of Play*. Harmondsworth: Penguin.

National Autistic Society (2020, August 14) *Sleep - a guide for parents of autistic children*. National Autistic Society. Accessed on 04/05/2022 at www.autism.org.uk/advice-and-guidance/topics/physical-health/ sleep/parents.

NHS (2019, November 8) *Melatonin for sleep problems*. NHS. Accessed on 04/05/2022 at www.nhs.uk/medicines/melatonin.

NHS (2021, February 12) *Overview – Eating disorders*. NHS. Accessed on 04/05/2022 at www.nhs.uk/mental-health/ feelings-symptoms-behaviours/behaviours/eating-disorders/ overview.

Spence, C. (2015a) Just how much of what we taste derives from the sense of smell? *Flavour*, 4(30) https://doi.org/10.1186/s13411-015-0040-2.

Spence, C. (2015b) On the psychological impact of food colour? *Flavour*, 4(21) https://doi.org/10.1186/s13411-015-0031-3.

Stock Kranowitz, C. (2005) *The Out-of-Sync Child*. New York: Penguin.

Index